Looking for Pythagoras

The Pythagorean Theorem

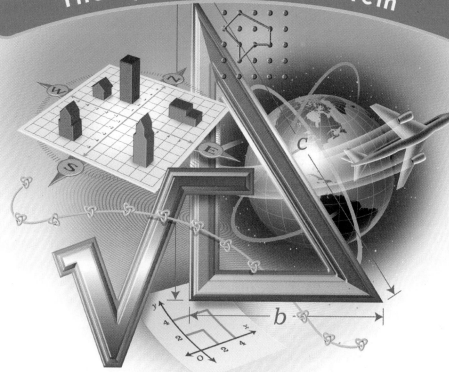

Glenda Lappan

James T. Fey

William M. Fitzgerald

Susan N. Friel

Elizabeth Difanis Phillips

Boston, Massachusetts · Glenview, Illinois · Shoreview, Minnesota · Upper Saddle River, New Jersey

Connected Mathematics™ was developed at Michigan State University with financial support from the Michigan State University Office of the Provost, Computing and Technology, and the College of Natural Science.

This material is based upon work supported by the National Science Foundation under Grant No. MDR 9150217 and Grant No. ESI 9986372. Opinions expressed are those of the authors and not necessarily those of the Foundation.

The Michigan State University authors and administration have agreed that all MSU royalties arising from this publication will be devoted to purposes supported by the MSU Mathematics Education Enrichment Fund.

Acknowledgments appear on page 74, which constitutes an extension of this copyright page.

13-digit ISBN 978-0-13-366150-7
10-digit ISBN 0-13-366150-4
1 2 3 4 5 6 7 8 9 10   11 10 09 08

Authors of Connected Mathematics

(from left to right) Glenda Lappan, Betty Phillips, Susan Friel, Bill Fitzgerald, Jim Fey

Glenda Lappan is a University Distinguished Professor in the Department of Mathematics at Michigan State University. Her research and development interests are in the connected areas of students' learning of mathematics and mathematics teachers' professional growth and change related to the development and enactment of K–12 curriculum materials.

James T. Fey is a Professor of Curriculum and Instruction and Mathematics at the University of Maryland. His consistent professional interest has been development and research focused on curriculum materials that engage middle and high school students in problem-based collaborative investigations of mathematical ideas and their applications.

William M. Fitzgerald *(Deceased)* was a Professor in the Department of Mathematics at Michigan State University. His early research was on the use of concrete materials in supporting student learning and led to the development of teaching materials for laboratory environments. Later he helped develop a teaching model to support student experimentation with mathematics.

Susan N. Friel is a Professor of Mathematics Education in the School of Education at the University of North Carolina at Chapel Hill. Her research interests focus on statistics education for middle-grade students and, more broadly, on teachers' professional development and growth in teaching mathematics K–8.

Elizabeth Difanis Phillips is a Senior Academic Specialist in the Mathematics Department of Michigan State University. She is interested in teaching and learning mathematics for both teachers and students. These interests have led to curriculum and professional development projects at the middle school and high school levels, as well as projects related to the teaching and learning of algebra across the grades.

CMP2 Development Staff

Teacher Collaborator in Residence
Yvonne Grant
Michigan State University

Administrative Assistant
Judith Martus Miller
Michigan State University

Production and Field Site Manager
Lisa Keller
Michigan State University

Technical and Editorial Support
**Brin Keller, Peter Lappan, Jim Laser,
Michael Masterson, Stacey Miceli**

Assessment Team
June Bailey and **Debra Sobko** (Apollo Middle School, Rochester, New York), **George Bright** (University of North Carolina, Greensboro), **Gwen Ranzau Campbell** (Sunrise Park Middle School, White Bear Lake, Minnesota), **Holly DeRosia, Kathy Dole,** and **Teri Keusch** (Portland Middle School, Portland, Michigan), **Mary Beth Schmitt** (Traverse City East Junior High School, Traverse City, Michigan), **Genni Steele** (Central Middle School, White Bear Lake, Minnesota), **Jacqueline Stewart** (Okemos, Michigan), **Elizabeth Tye** (Magnolia Junior High School, Magnolia, Arkansas)

Development Assistants
At Lansing Community College *Undergraduate Assistant:* **James Brinegar**

At Michigan State University *Graduate Assistants:* **Dawn Berk, Emily Bouck, Bulent Buyukbozkirli, Kuo-Liang Chang, Christopher Danielson, Srinivasa Dharmavaram, Deb Johanning, Wesley Kretzschmar, Kelly Rivette, Sarah Sword, Tat Ming Sze, Marie Turini, Jeffrey Wanko;** *Undergraduate Assistants:* **Daniel Briggs, Jeffrey Chapin, Jade Corsé, Elisha Hardy, Alisha Harold, Elizabeth Keusch, Julia Letoutchaia, Karen Loeffler, Brian Oliver, Carl Oliver, Evonne Pedawi, Lauren Rebrovich**

At the University of Maryland *Graduate Assistants:* **Kim Harris Bethea, Kara Karch**

At the University of North Carolina (Chapel Hill) *Graduate Assistants:* **Mark Ellis, Trista Stearns;** *Undergraduate Assistant:* **Daniel Smith**

Advisory Board for CMP2

Thomas Banchoff
Professor of Mathematics
Brown University
Providence, Rhode Island

Anne Bartel
Mathematics Coordinator
Minneapolis Public Schools
Minneapolis, Minnesota

Hyman Bass
Professor of Mathematics
University of Michigan
Ann Arbor, Michigan

Joan Ferrini-Mundy
Associate Dean of the College of
Natural Science; Professor
Michigan State University
East Lansing, Michigan

James Hiebert
Professor
University of Delaware
Newark, Delaware

Susan Hudson Hull
Charles A. Dana Center
University of Texas
Austin, Texas

Michele Luke
Mathematics Curriculum
Coordinator
West Junior High
Minnetonka, Minnesota

Kay McClain
Assistant Professor of
Mathematics Education
Vanderbilt University
Nashville, Tennessee

Edward Silver
Professor; Chair of Educational
Studies
University of Michigan
Ann Arbor, Michigan

Judith Sowder
Professor Emerita
San Diego State University
San Diego, California

Lisa Usher
Mathematics Resource Teacher
California Academy of
Mathematics and Science
San Pedro, California

Field Test Sites for CMP2

During the development of the revised edition of *Connected Mathematics* (CMP2), more than 100 classroom teachers have field-tested materials at 49 school sites in 12 states and the District of Columbia. This classroom testing occurred over three academic years (2001 through 2004), allowing careful study of the effectiveness of each of the 24 units that comprise the program. A special thanks to the students and teachers at these pilot schools.

Arkansas
Magnolia Public Schools
Kittena Bell*, Judith Trowell*; *Central Elementary School:* Maxine Broom, Betty Eddy, Tiffany Fallin, Bonnie Flurry, Carolyn Monk, Elizabeth Tye; *Magnolia Junior High School:* Monique Bryan, Ginger Cook, David Graham, Shelby Lamkin

Colorado
Boulder Public Schools
Nevin Platt Middle School: Judith Koenig
St. Vrain Valley School District, Longmont
Westview Middle School: Colleen Beyer, Kitty Canupp, Ellie Decker*, Peggy McCarthy, Tanya deNobrega, Cindy Payne, Ericka Pilon, Andrew Roberts

District of Columbia
Capitol Hill Day School: Ann Lawrence

Georgia
University of Georgia, Athens
Brad Findell
Madison Public Schools
Morgan County Middle School: Renee Burgdorf, Lynn Harris, Nancy Kurtz, Carolyn Stewart

Maine
Falmouth Public Schools
Falmouth Middle School: Donna Erikson, Joyce Hebert, Paula Hodgkins, Rick Hogan, David Legere, Cynthia Martin, Barbara Stiles, Shawn Towle*

Michigan
Portland Public Schools
Portland Middle School: Mark Braun, Holly DeRosia, Kathy Dole*, Angie Foote, Teri Keusch, Tammi Wardwell
Traverse City Area Public Schools
Bertha Vos Elementary: Kristin Sak; *Central Grade School:* Michelle Clark; Jody Meyers; *Eastern Elementary:* Karrie Tufts; *Interlochen Elementary:* Mary McGee-Cullen; *Long Lake Elementary:* Julie Faulkner*, Charlie Maxbauer, Katherine Sleder; *Norris Elementary:* Hope Slanaker; *Oak Park Elementary:* Jessica Steed; *Traverse Heights Elementary:* Jennifer Wolfert; *Westwoods Elementary:* Nancy Conn; *Old Mission Peninsula School:* Deb Larimer; *Traverse City East Junior High:* Ivanka Berkshire, Ruthanne Kladder, Jan Palkowski, Jane Peterson, Mary Beth Schmitt; *Traverse City West Junior High:* Dan Fouch*, Ray Fouch
Sturgis Public Schools
Sturgis Middle School: Ellen Eisele

Minnesota
Burnsville School District 191
Hidden Valley Elementary: Stephanie Cin, Jane McDevitt
Hopkins School District 270
Alice Smith Elementary: Sandra Cowing, Kathleen Gustafson, Martha Mason, Scott Stillman; *Eisenhower Elementary:* Chad Bellig, Patrick Berger, Nancy Glades, Kye Johnson, Shane Wasserman, Victoria Wilson; *Gatewood Elementary:* Sarah Ham, Julie Kloos, Janine Pung, Larry Wade; *Glen Lake Elementary:* Jacqueline Cramer, Kathy Hering, Cecelia Morris,

Robb Trenda; *Katherine Curren Elementary:* Diane Bancroft, Sue DeWit, John Wilson; *L. H. Tanglen Elementary:* Kevin Athmann, Lisa Becker, Mary LaBelle, Kathy Rezac, Roberta Severson; *Meadowbrook Elementary:* Jan Gauger, Hildy Shank, Jessica Zimmerman; *North Junior High:* Laurel Hahn, Kristin Lee, Jodi Markuson, Bruce Mestemacher, Laurel Miller, Bonnie Rinker, Jeannine Salzer, Sarah Shafer, Cam Stottler; *West Junior High:* Alicia Beebe, Kristie Earl, Nobu Fujii, Pam Georgetti, Susan Gilbert, Regina Nelson Johnson, Debra Lindstrom, Michele Luke*, Jon Sorenson
Minneapolis School District 1
Ann Sullivan K-8 School: Bronwyn Collins; Anne Bartel* (Curriculum and Instruction Office)
Wayzata School District 284
Central Middle School: Sarajane Myers, Dan Nielsen, Tanya Ravenholdt
White Bear Lake School District 624
Central Middle School: Amy Jorgenson, Michelle Reich, Brenda Sammon

New York
New York City Public Schools
IS 89: Yelena Aynbinder, Chi-Man Ng, Nina Rapaport, Joel Spengler, Phyllis Tam*, Brent Wyso; *Wagner Middle School:* Jason Appel, Intissar Fernandez, Yee Gee Get, Richard Goldstein, Irving Marcus, Sue Norton, Bernadita Owens, Jennifer Rehn*, Kevin Yuhas

---

* indicates a Field Test Site Coordinator

Ohio

Talawanda School District, Oxford
Talawanda Middle School: Teresa Abrams, Larry Brock, Heather Brosey, Julie Churchman, Monna Even, Karen Fitch, Bob George, Amanda Klee, Pat Meade, Sandy Montgomery, Barbara Sherman, Lauren Steidl

Miami University
Jeffrey Wanko*

Springfield Public Schools
Rockway School: Jim Mamer

Pennsylvania

Pittsburgh Public Schools
Kenneth Labuskes, Marianne O'Connor, Mary Lynn Raith*; *Arthur J. Rooney Middle School:* David Hairston, Stamatina Mousetis, Alfredo Zangaro; *Frick International Studies Academy:* Suzanne Berry, Janet Falkowski, Constance Finseth, Romika Hodge, Frank Machi; *Reizenstein Middle School:* Jeff Baldwin, James Brautigam, Lorena Burnett, Glen Cobbett, Michael Jordan, Margaret Lazur, Melissa Munnell, Holly Neely, Ingrid Reed, Dennis Reft

Texas

Austin Independent School District
Bedichek Middle School: Lisa Brown, Jennifer Glasscock, Vicki Massey

El Paso Independent School District
Cordova Middle School: Armando Aguirre, Anneliesa Durkes, Sylvia Guzman, Pat Holguin*, William Holguin, Nancy Nava, Laura Orozco, Michelle Peña, Roberta Rosen, Patsy Smith, Jeremy Wolf

Plano Independent School District
Patt Henry, James Wohlgehagen*; *Frankford Middle School:* Mandy Baker, Cheryl Butsch, Amy Dudley, Betsy Eshelman, Janet Greene, Cort Haynes, Kathy Letchworth, Kay Marshall, Kelly McCants, Amy Reck, Judy Scott, Syndy Snyder, Lisa Wang; *Wilson Middle School:* Darcie Bane, Amanda Bedenko, Whitney Evans, Tonelli Hatley, Sarah (Becky) Higgs, Kelly Johnston, Rebecca McElligott, Kay Neuse, Cheri Slocum, Kelli Straight

Washington

Evergreen School District
Shahala Middle School: Nicole Abrahamsen, Terry Coon*, Carey Doyle, Sheryl Drechsler, George Gemma, Gina Helland, Amy Hilario, Darla Lidyard, Sean McCarthy, Tilly Meyer, Willow Neuwelt, Todd Parsons, Brian Pederson, Stan Posey, Shawn Scott, Craig Sjoberg, Lynette Sundstrom, Charles Switzer, Luke Youngblood

Wisconsin

Beaver Dam Unified School District
Beaver Dam Middle School: Jim Braemer, Jeanne Frick, Jessica Greatens, Barbara Link, Dennis McCormick, Karen Michels, Nancy Nichols*, Nancy Palm, Shelly Stelsel, Susan Wiggins

---

* indicates a Field Test Site Coordinator

Reviews of CMP to Guide Development of CMP2

Before writing for CMP2 began or field tests were conducted, the first edition of *Connected Mathematics* was submitted to the mathematics faculties of school districts from many parts of the country and to 80 individual reviewers for extensive comments.

School District Survey Reviews of CMP

Arizona
Madison School District #38 (Phoenix)

Arkansas
Cabot School District, Little Rock School District, Magnolia School District

California
Los Angeles Unified School District

Colorado
St. Vrain Valley School District (Longmont)

Florida
Leon County Schools (Tallahassee)

Illinois
School District #21 (Wheeling)

Indiana
Joseph L. Block Junior High (East Chicago)

Kentucky
Fayette County Public Schools (Lexington)

Maine
Selection of Schools

Massachusetts
Selection of Schools

Michigan
Sparta Area Schools

Minnesota
Hopkins School District

Texas
Austin Independent School District, The El Paso Collaborative for Academic Excellence, Plano Independent School District

Wisconsin
Platteville Middle School

Individual Reviewers of CMP

Arkansas
Deborah Cramer; Robby Frizzell *(Taylor)*; Lowell Lynde *(University of Arkansas, Monticello)*; Leigh Manzer *(Norfork)*; Lynne Roberts *(Emerson High School, Emerson)*; Tony Timms *(Cabot Public Schools)*; Judith Trowell *(Arkansas Department of Higher Education)*

California
José Alcantar *(Gilroy)*; Eugenie Belcher *(Gilroy)*; Marian Pasternack *(Lowman M. S. T. Center, North Hollywood)*; Susana Pezoa *(San Jose)*; Todd Rabusin *(Hollister)*; Margaret Siegfried *(Ocala Middle School, San Jose)*; Polly Underwood *(Ocala Middle School, San Jose)*

Colorado
Janeane Golliher *(St. Vrain Valley School District, Longmont)*; Judith Koenig *(Nevin Platt Middle School, Boulder)*

Florida
Paige Loggins *(Swift Creek Middle School, Tallahassee)*

Illinois
Jan Robinson *(School District #21, Wheeling)*

Indiana
Frances Jackson *(Joseph L. Block Junior High, East Chicago)*

Kentucky
Natalee Feese *(Fayette County Public Schools, Lexington)*

Maine
Betsy Berry *(Maine Math & Science Alliance, Augusta)*

Maryland
Joseph Gagnon *(University of Maryland, College Park)*; Paula Maccini *(University of Maryland, College Park)*

Massachusetts
George Cobb *(Mt. Holyoke College, South Hadley)*; Cliff Kanold *(University of Massachusetts, Amherst)*

Michigan
Mary Bouck *(Farwell Area Schools)*; Carol Dorer *(Slauson Middle School, Ann Arbor)*; Carrie Heaney *(Forsythe Middle School, Ann Arbor)*; Ellen Hopkins *(Clague Middle School, Ann Arbor)*; Teri Keusch *(Portland Middle School, Portland)*; Valerie Mills *(Oakland Schools, Waterford)*; Mary Beth Schmitt *(Traverse City East Junior High, Traverse City)*; Jack Smith *(Michigan State University, East Lansing)*; Rebecca Spencer *(Sparta Middle School, Sparta)*; Ann Marie Nicoll Turner *(Tappan Middle School, Ann Arbor)*; Scott Turner *(Scarlett Middle School, Ann Arbor)*

Minnesota
Margarita Alvarez *(Olson Middle School, Minneapolis)*; Jane Amundson *(Nicollet Junior High, Burnsville)*; Anne Bartel *(Minneapolis Public Schools)*; Gwen Ranzau Campbell *(Sunrise Park Middle School, White Bear Lake)*; Stephanie Cin *(Hidden Valley Elementary, Burnsville)*; Joan Garfield *(University of Minnesota, Minneapolis)*; Gretchen Hall *(Richfield Middle School, Richfield)*; Jennifer Larson *(Olson Middle School, Minneapolis)*; Michele Luke *(West Junior High, Minnetonka)*; Jeni Meyer *(Richfield Junior High, Richfield)*; Judy Pfingsten *(Inver Grove Heights Middle School, Inver Grove Heights)*; Sarah Shafer *(North Junior High, Minnetonka)*; Genni Steele *(Central Middle School, White Bear Lake)*; Victoria Wilson *(Eisenhower Elementary, Hopkins)*; Paul Zorn *(St. Olaf College, Northfield)*

New York
Debra Altenau-Bartolino *(Greenwich Village Middle School, New York)*; Doug Clements *(University of Buffalo)*; Francis Curcio *(New York University, New York)*; Christine Dorosh *(Clinton School for Writers, Brooklyn)*; Jennifer Rehn *(East Side Middle School, New York)*; Phyllis Tam *(IS 89 Lab School, New York)*;

Marie Turini *(Louis Armstrong Middle School, New York)*; Lucy West *(Community School District 2, New York)*; Monica Witt *(Simon Baruch Intermediate School 104, New York)*

Pennsylvania
Robert Aglietti *(Pittsburgh)*; Sharon Mihalich *(Pittsburgh)*; Jennifer Plumb *(South Hills Middle School, Pittsburgh)*; Mary Lynn Raith *(Pittsburgh Public Schools)*

Texas
Michelle Bittick *(Austin Independent School District)*; Margaret Cregg *(Plano Independent School District)*; Sheila Cunningham *(Klein Independent School District)*; Judy Hill *(Austin Independent School District)*; Patricia Holguin *(El Paso Independent School District)*; Bonnie McNemar *(Arlington)*; Kay Neuse *(Plano Independent School District)*; Joyce Polanco *(Austin Independent School District)*; Marge Ramirez *(University of Texas at El Paso)*; Pat Rossman *(Baker Campus, Austin)*; Cindy Schimek *(Houston)*; Cynthia Schneider *(Charles A. Dana Center, University of Texas at Austin)*; Uri Treisman *(Charles A. Dana Center, University of Texas at Austin)*; Jacqueline Weilmuenster *(Grapevine-Colleyville Independent School District)*; LuAnn Weynand *(San Antonio)*; Carmen Whitman *(Austin Independent School District)*; James Wohlgehagen *(Plano Independent School District)*

Washington
Ramesh Gangolli *(University of Washington, Seattle)*

Wisconsin
Susan Lamon *(Marquette University, Hales Corner)*; Steve Reinhart *(retired, Chippewa Falls Middle School, Eau Claire)*

Table of Contents

Looking for Pythagoras
The Pythagorean Theorem

Looking for Pythagoras

Suppose you are planning an airplane trip to several cities in your state. What types of information would you need to give the pilot so he would know where to go?

To mark the square corners of their property, ancient Egyptians used a rope divided by knots into 12 equal segments. How do you think they used this tool?

On a standard baseball diamond, the bases are 90 feet apart. How far must a catcher at home plate throw the ball to get a runner out at second base?

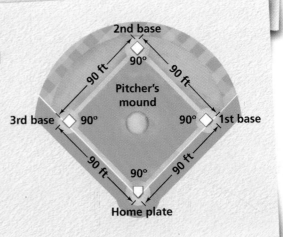

In this unit, you will explore side lengths and areas of right triangles and squares. Your explorations will lead you to discover one of the most important relationships in all of mathematics: the *Pythagorean Theorem*. The Pythagorean Theorem is so important that much of geometry, trigonometry, and calculus would be impossible without it.

In your previous work, you used whole numbers and fractions to describe lengths. In this unit, you will work with lengths that are impossible to describe with whole numbers or fractions. To talk about such lengths, you need to use another type of number, called an *irrational number.*

As you work on this unit, you will use what you are learning to solve problems like those on the previous page.

Mathematical Highlights

The Pythagorean Theorem

In *Looking for Pythagoras,* you will explore an important relationship among the side lengths of a right triangle.

You will learn how to

- Relate the area of a square to its side length
- Develop strategies for finding the distance between two points on a coordinate grid
- Understand and apply the Pythagorean Theorem
- Estimate the values of square roots of whole numbers
- Use the Pythagorean Theorem to solve everyday problems
- Locate irrational numbers on a number line

As you work on problems in this unit, ask yourself questions about problem situations that involve right triangles:

Is it appropriate and useful to use the Pythagorean Theorem in this situation? How do I know this?

Do I need to find the distance between two points?

How are irrational numbers and areas of squares related?

How can I estimate the square root of a number?

How can I find the length of something without directly measuring it?

Coordinate Grids

In this investigation, you will review how to use a coordinate grid to locate points in the plane. You will then explore how to find distances between points and areas of figures on a coordinate grid.

In the first two problems of this investigation, the coordinate grid is in the form of a street map of a fictional city called Euclid. The streets in most cities do not form perfect coordinate grids as they do in Euclid. However, many cities have streets that are at least loosely based on a coordinate system. One well-known example is Washington, D.C.

Did You Know?

The Lincoln Memorial stands at the west end of the National Mall in Washington, D.C. Built between 1914 and 1922, the memorial houses a 99-foot-tall statue of the first Republican president, Abraham Lincoln. The memorial celebrates Lincoln's accomplishments in uniting the divided nation and his quest to end slavery.

People often make speeches at the Lincoln Memorial, using the setting to strengthen their message. Martin Luther King, Jr. gave his famous "I have a Dream" speech at the memorial during the March on Washington in 1963.

Go Online
PHSchool.com

For: Information about the Lincoln Memorial
Web Code: ape-9031

The map on the next page shows the central part of Washington, D.C. The city's street system was designed by Pierre L'Enfant in 1791.

L'Enfant's design is based on a coordinate system. Here are some key features of L'Enfant's system:

- The north-south and east-west streets form grid lines.
- The origin is at the Capitol.
- The vertical axis is formed by North and South Capitol Streets.
- The horizontal axis is the line stretching from the Lincoln Memorial, through the Mall, and down East Capitol Street.
- The axes divide the city into four quadrants known as Northeast (NE), Southeast (SE), Southwest (SW), and Northwest (NW).

- Describe the locations of these landmarks:

  George Washington University

  Dupont Circle

  Benjamin Banneker Park

  The White House

  Union Station

- How can you find the distance from Union Station to Dupont Circle?

- Find the intersection of G Street and 8th Street SE and the intersection of G Street and 8th Street NW. How are these locations related to the Capitol Building?

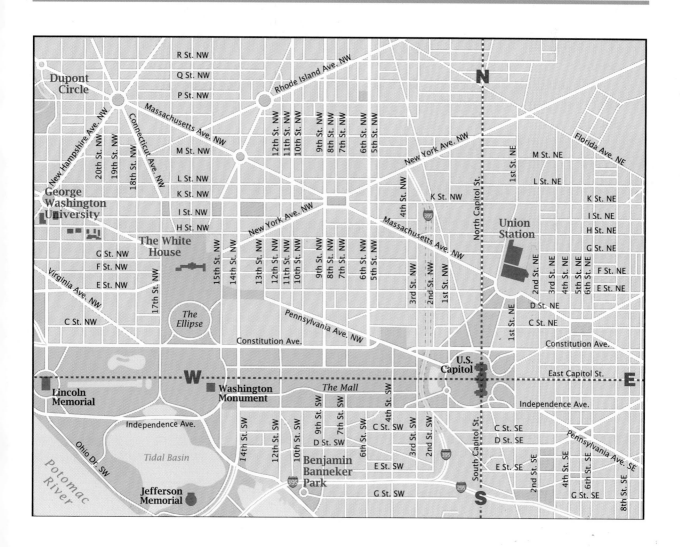

In mathematics, we use a coordinate system to describe the locations of points. Recall that horizontal and vertical number lines, called the *x*- and *y*-axes, divide the plane into four quadrants.

You describe the location of a point by giving its coordinates as an ordered pair of the form (*x*, *y*). On the coordinate grid at the right, four points are labeled with their coordinates.

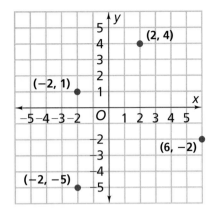

Driving Around Euclid

1.1

The founders of the city of Euclid loved math. They named their city after a famous mathematician, and they designed the street system to look like a coordinate grid. The Euclideans describe the locations of buildings and other landmarks by giving coordinates. For example, the art museum is located at (6, 1).

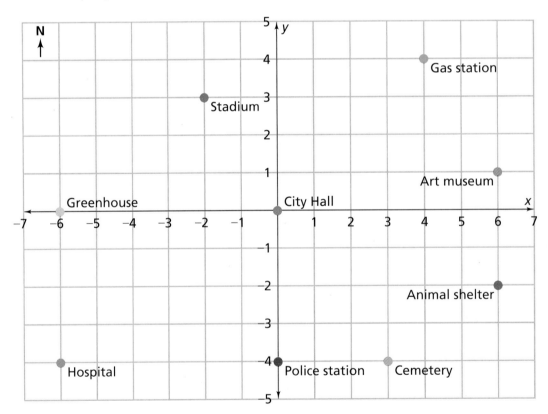

A. Give the coordinates of each landmark.

   1. gas station

   2. animal shelter

   3. stadium

B. Euclid's chief of police is planning emergency routes. She needs to find the shortest driving route between the following pairs of locations:

Pair 1: the police station to City Hall

Pair 2: the hospital to City Hall

Pair 3: the hospital to the art museum

   1. Give precise directions for an emergency car route for each pair.

   2. For each pair, find the total distance in blocks a police car following your route would travel.

C. Suppose you know the coordinates of two landmarks in Euclid. How can you determine the shortest driving distance (in blocks) between them?

D. A helicopter can travel directly from one point to another. For each pair in Question B, find the total distance (in blocks) a helicopter would have to travel to get from the starting location to the ending location. You may find it helpful to use a centimeter ruler.

E. Will a direct helicopter route between two locations always be shorter than a car route? Explain your reasoning.

ACE **Homework starts on page 12.**

The Euclid City Council is developing parks with geometric shapes. For some of the parks, the council gives the park designers constraints. For example, Descartes Park must have a border with vertices $(1, 1)$ and $(4, 2)$.

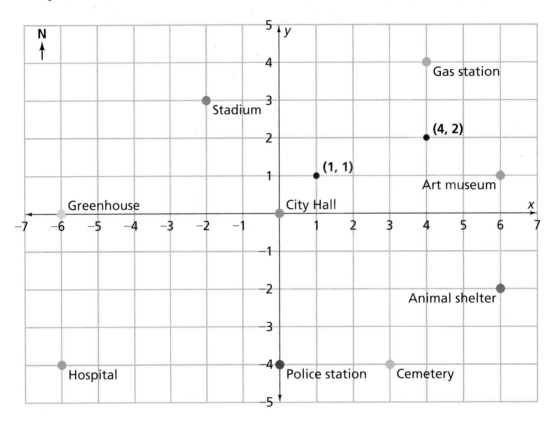

Problem 1.2 Shapes on a Coordinate Grid

Be prepared to explain your answers.

A. Suppose the park is to be a square. What could the coordinates of the other two vertices be? Give two answers.

B. Suppose the park is to be a nonsquare rectangle. What could the coordinates of the other two vertices be?

C. Suppose the park is to be a right triangle. What could the coordinates of the other vertex be?

D. Suppose the park is to be a parallelogram that is not a rectangle. What could the coordinates of the other two vertices be?

ACE Homework starts on page 12.

1.3 Finding Areas

Below are some park designs submitted to the Euclid City Council. To determine costs, the council needs to know the area of each park.

1. 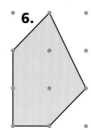 2. 3. 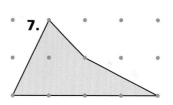 4.

5. 6. 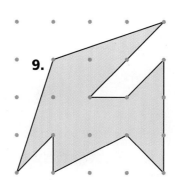 7.

8. 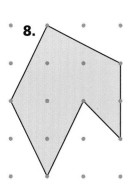 9. 10.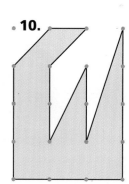

Problem 1.3 Finding Areas

Consider the horizontal or vertical distance between two adjacent dots to be 1 unit.

A. Find the area of each figure.

B. Find the area of one of the square parks you suggested in Problem 1.2.

C. Describe the strategies you used in Questions A and B.

ACE Homework starts on page 12.

active math online

For: Dynamic Geoboard
Visit: PHSchool.com
Web Code: apd-2100

Applications

For Exercises 1–7, use the map of Euclid from Problem 1.1.

1. Give the coordinates of each landmark.

    a. art museum   **b.** hospital   **c.** greenhouse

2. What is the shortest driving distance from the animal shelter to the stadium?

3. What is the shortest driving distance from the hospital to the gas station?

4. What are the coordinates of a point halfway from City Hall to the hospital if you travel by taxi? Is there more than one possibility? Explain.

5. What are the coordinates of a point halfway from City Hall to the hospital if you travel by helicopter? Is there more than one possibility? Explain.

6. a. Which landmarks are 7 blocks from City Hall by car?

    b. Give precise driving directions from City Hall to each landmark you listed in part (a).

7. Euclid Middle School is located at the intersection of two streets. The school is the same driving distance from the gas station as the hospital is from the greenhouse.

    a. List the coordinates of each place on the map where the school might be located.

    b. Find the flying distance, in blocks, from the gas station to each location you listed in part (a).

The points (0, 0) and (3, 2) are two vertices of a polygon with integer coordinates.

Homework
Help Online
PHSchool.com
For: Help with Exercise 8
Web Code: ape-2108

8. What could the other two vertices be if the polygon is a square?

9. Suppose the polygon is a nonrectangular parallelogram. What could the other two vertices be?

10. What could the other vertex be if the polygon is a right triangle?

The points (3, 3) and (2, 6) are two vertices of a right triangle. Use this information for Exercises 11–13.

11. **Multiple Choice** Which point could be the third vertex of the right triangle?

    A. (3, 2)   **B.** (−1, 5)   **C.** (7, 4)   **D.** (0, 3)

12. Give the coordinates of at least two other points that could be the third vertex.

13. How many right triangles with vertices (3, 3) and (2, 6) can you draw? Explain.

14. Can the following points be connected to form a parallelogram? Explain.

    (1, 1)   (2, −2)   (4, 2)   (3, 5)

Find the area of each triangle. Copy the triangles onto dot paper if you need to.

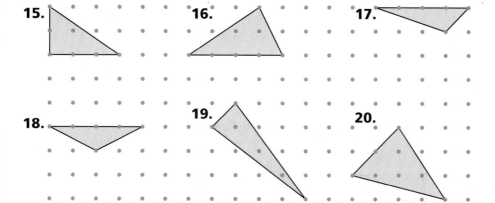

15.

16.

17.

18.

19.

20.

Applications

Find the area of each figure, and describe the method you use. Copy the figures onto dot paper if you need to.

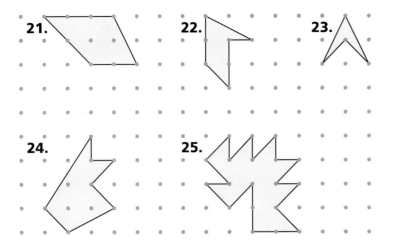

21.

22.

23.

24.

25.

Connections

In the city of Euclid, the length of each block is 150 meters. Use this information and the map from Problem 1.1 for Exercises 26–28.

26. What is the shortest driving distance, in meters, from City Hall to the animal shelter?

27. What is the shortest driving distance, in meters, from the police station to the gas station?

28. Between which two landmarks is the shortest driving distance 750 meters?

29. When she solved Problem 1.2, Fabiola used slopes to help explain her answers.

   a. In Question A, she used slopes to show that adjacent sides of the figure were perpendicular. How might she have done this?

   b. In Question D, she used slopes to show that the figure was a parallelogram. How might she have done this?

30. Refer to the map of Euclid from Problem 1.1.

    a. Matsu walks 2 blocks west from the police station and then walks 3 blocks north. Give the coordinates of the place where he stops.

    b. Matsu's friend Cassandra is at City Hall. She wants to meet Matsu at his ending location from part (a). What is the shortest route she can take if she walks along city streets? Is there more than one possible shortest route?

    c. Lei leaves the stadium and walks 3 blocks east, then 3 blocks south, then 2 blocks west, and finally 4 blocks north. Give the coordinates of the place where she stops.

    d. Lei's sister Aida wants to meet her at her ending location from part (c). Aida is now at City Hall. What is the shortest route she can take if she walks along city streets? Is there more than one possible shortest route?

    e. In general, how can you find the shortest route, walking along city streets, from City Hall to any point in Euclid?

31. Below are equations for eight lines.

line 1: $y = 3x + 5$ line 2: $y = 0.5x + 3$
line 3: $y = 10 - 2x$ line 4: $y = 1 - \frac{1}{3}x$
line 5: $y = 7 + 3x$ line 6: $y = -2x + 1$
line 7: $y = 5 + 6x$ line 8: $y = 3x$

Go Online
PHSchool.com
For: Multiple-Choice Skills
Practice
Web Code: apa-2154

a. Which of the lines are parallel to each other?

b. Which of the lines are perpendicular to each other?

32. Marcia finds the area of a figure on dot paper by dividing it into smaller shapes. She finds the area of each smaller shape and writes the sum of the areas as $\frac{1}{2} \cdot 3 + \frac{1}{2} + \frac{1}{2} + 1$.

a. What is the total area of the figure?

b. On dot paper, draw a figure Marcia might have been looking at.

33. In the figure, a circle is inscribed in a square.

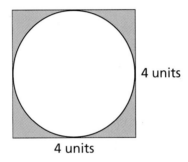

4 units

4 units

a. Find the area of the circle.

b. Find the area of the shaded region.

34. Refer to the ordered pairs to answer the questions. Do *not* plot the points on a grid. Explain each answer.

$(2, -3)$ $(3, -4)$ $(-4, -5)$ $(4, 5)$
$(-4, 6)$ $(-5, -5)$ $(0, -6)$ $(6, 0)$

a. Which point is farthest right?

b. Which point is farthest left?

c. Which point is above the others?

d. Which point is below the others?

Extensions

35. Find a road map of your city or county. Figure out how to use the map's index to locate a city, street, or other landmark. How is finding a landmark by using an index description similar to and different from finding a landmark in Euclid by using its coordinates?

36. Use a map of your state to plan an airplane trip from your city or town to four other locations in your state. Write a set of directions for your trip that you could give to the pilot.

37. On grid paper, draw several parallelograms with diagonals that are perpendicular to each other. What do you observe about these parallelograms?

38. Find the areas of triangles *AST, BST, CST,* and *DST*. How do the areas compare? Why do you think this is true?

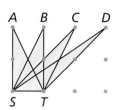

39. Find the areas of triangles *VMN, WMN, XMN, YMN,* and *ZMN*. How do the areas compare? Why do you think this is true?

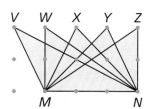

Mathematical Reflections 1

In this investigation, you solved problems involving coordinate grids. You located points, calculated distances and areas, and found vertices of polygons that satisfied given conditions. The following questions will help you summarize what you have learned.

Think about your answers to these questions. Discuss your ideas with other students and your teacher. Then write a summary of your findings in your notebook.

1. In the city of Euclid, how does the driving distance from one place to another compare to the flying distance?

2. Suppose you know the coordinates of two landmarks in Euclid. How can you find the distance between the landmarks?

3. Describe some strategies you can use to find areas of figures drawn on dot paper. Give examples if it helps you explain your thinking.

Investigation 2

Squaring Off

In this investigation, you will explore the relationship between the side lengths and areas of squares and use that relationship to find the lengths of segments on dot grids.

2.1 Looking for Squares

You can draw squares with different areas by connecting the points on a 5 dot-by-5 dot grid. Two simple examples follow.

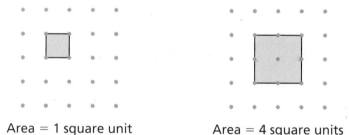

Area = 1 square unit   Area = 4 square units

In this problem, you will explore other possible areas.

Problem 2.1 Looking for Squares

A. On 5 dot-by-5 dot grids, draw squares of various sizes by connecting dots. Draw squares with as many different areas as possible Label each square with its area. Include at least one square whose sides are not horizontal and vertical.

B. Analyze your set of squares and describe the side lengths you found.

ACE Homework starts on page 23.

The area of a square is the length of a side multiplied by itself. This can be expressed by the formula $A = s \cdot s$, or $A = s^2$.

If you know the area of a square, you can work backward to find the length of a side. For example, suppose a square has an area of 4 square units. To find the length of a side, you need to figure out what positive number multiplied by itself equals 4. Because $2 \cdot 2 = 4$, the side length is 2 units. We call 2 a **square root** of 4.

This square has an area of 4 square units. The length of each side is the square root of 4, or 2, units.

In general, if $A = s^2$, then s is a square root of A. Because $2 \cdot 2 = 4$ and $-2 \cdot -2 = 4$, 2 and -2 are both square roots of 4. Every positive number has two square roots. The number 0 has only one square root, 0.

If N is a positive number, then $\sqrt{N}$ indicates the positive square root of N. For example, $\sqrt{4} = 2$. The negative square root of 4 is $-\sqrt{4} = -2$.

If the area of a square is known, then square roots can be used to describe the length of a side of the square.

The area of a square is the side length squared.

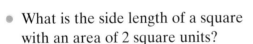

Getting Ready for Problem 2.2

- What is the side length of a square with an area of 2 square units?
- Is this length greater than 1? Is it greater than 2?
- Is 1.5 a good estimate for $\sqrt{2}$?
- Can you find a better estimate for $\sqrt{2}$?

In this problem, use your calculator only when the question directs you to.

A. 1. Find the side lengths of squares with areas of 1, 9, 16, and 25 square units.

   2. Find the values of $\sqrt{1}$, $\sqrt{9}$, $\sqrt{16}$, and $\sqrt{25}$.

B. 1. What is the area of a square with a side length of 12 units? What is the area of a square with a side length of 2.5 units?

   2. Find the missing numbers.

$$\sqrt{\blacksquare} = 12 \qquad \sqrt{\blacksquare} = 2.5$$

C. Refer to the square with an area of 2 square units you drew in Problem 2.1. The exact side length of this square is $\sqrt{2}$ units.

   1. Estimate $\sqrt{2}$ by measuring a side of the square with a centimeter ruler.

   2. Calculate the area of the square, using your measurement from part (1). Is the result exactly equal to 2?

   3. Use the square root key on your calculator to estimate $\sqrt{2}$.

   4. How does your ruler estimate compare to your calculator estimate?

D. 1. Which two whole numbers is $\sqrt{5}$ between? Explain.

   2. Which whole number is closer to $\sqrt{5}$? Explain.

   3. Without using the square root key on your calculator, estimate the value of $\sqrt{5}$ to two decimal places.

E. Give the exact side length of each square you drew in Problem 2.1.

ACE Homework starts on page 23.

You can use a square to find the length of a segment connecting dots on a grid. For example, to find the length of the segment on the left, draw a square with the segment as a side. The square has an area of 5 square units, so the segment has length $\sqrt{5}$ units.

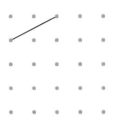 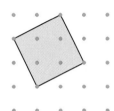

Problem 2.3 Using Squares to Find Lengths

A. 1. On 5 dot-by-5 dot grids, draw line segments with as many different lengths as possible by connecting dots. Label each segment with its length. Use the $\sqrt{}$ symbol to express lengths that are not whole numbers. (**Hint:** You will need to draw squares that extend beyond the 5-dot-by-5-dot grids.)

2. List the lengths in increasing order.

3. Estimate each non-whole number length to one decimal place.

B. Ella says the length of the segment at the left below is $\sqrt{8}$ units. Isabel says it is $2\sqrt{2}$ units. Are both students correct? Explain.

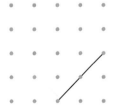 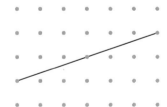

C. 1. Question B gives two ways of expressing the exact length of a segment. Express the exact length of the segment at the right above in two ways.

2. Can you find a segment whose length cannot be expressed in two ways as in Question B?

ACE **Homework starts on page 23.**

Applications

1. Find the area of every square that can be drawn by connecting dots on a 3 dot-by-3 dot grid.

2. On dot paper, draw a hexagon with an area of 16 square units.

3. On dot paper, draw a square with an area of 2 square units. Write an argument to convince a friend that the area is 2 square units.

4. Consider segment *AB* at right.

    a. On dot paper, draw a square with side *AB*. What is the area of the square?

    b. Use a calculator to estimate the length of segment *AB*.

5. Consider segment *CD* at right.

    a. On dot paper, draw a square with side *CD*. What is the area of the square?

    b. Use a calculator to estimate the length of segment *CD*.

6. Find the area and the side length of this square.

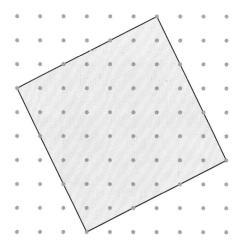

For Exercises 7–9, estimate each square root to one decimal place.

Go Online
PHSchool.com

For: Multiple-Choice Skills Practice
Web Code: apa-2254

7. $\sqrt{11}$ **8.** $\sqrt{30}$ **9.** $\sqrt{172}$

10. Multiple Choice Choose the pair of numbers $\sqrt{15}$ is between.

   A. 3.7 and 3.8   **B.** 3.8 and 3.9   **C.** 3.9 and 4.0   **D.** 14 and 16

Find exact values for each square root.

11. $\sqrt{144}$ **12.** $\sqrt{0.36}$ **13.** $\sqrt{961}$

Find the two consecutive whole numbers the square root is between. Explain.

14. $\sqrt{27}$ **15.** $\sqrt{1,000}$

Tell whether each statement is true.

16. $6 = \sqrt{36}$ **17.** $1.5 = \sqrt{2.25}$ **18.** $11 = \sqrt{101}$

Find the missing number.

19. $\sqrt{\blacksquare} = 81$ **20.** $14 = \sqrt{\blacksquare}$ **21.** $\blacksquare = \sqrt{28.09}$

22. $\sqrt{\blacksquare} = 3.2$ **23.** $\sqrt{\blacksquare} = \frac{1}{4}$ **24.** $\sqrt{\frac{4}{9}} = \blacksquare$

Find each product.

25. $\sqrt{2} \cdot \sqrt{2}$ **26.** $\sqrt{3} \cdot \sqrt{3}$ **27.** $\sqrt{4} \cdot \sqrt{4}$ **28.** $\sqrt{5} \cdot \sqrt{5}$

Give both the positive and negative square roots of each number.

29. 1   **30.** 4   **31.** 2

32. 16   **33.** 25   **34.** 5

Sorry, you can't use my square root key.

35. Find the length of every line segment that can be drawn by connecting dots on a 3 dot-by-3 dot grid.

Homework Help ◯nline
PHSchool.com
For: Help with Exercise 35
Web Code: ape-2235

36. Consider this segment.

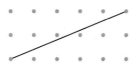

   a. Express the exact length of the segment, using the $\sqrt{\ }$ symbol.

   b. What two consecutive whole numbers is the length of the segment between?

37. Show that $2\sqrt{5}$ is equal to $\sqrt{20}$ by finding the length of line segment AC in two ways:

- Find the length of AB. Use the result to find the length of AC.
- Find the length of AC directly, as you did in Problem 2.3.

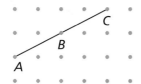

38. Multiple Choice Which line segment has a length of $\sqrt{17}$ units?

  F.

  G.

  H.

  J.

For Exercises 39 and 40, find the length of each side of the figure.

39.

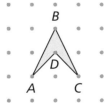

40.

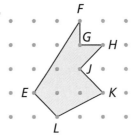

41. Put the following set of numbers in order on a number line.

| 2.3 | $2\frac{1}{4}$ | $\sqrt{5}$ | $\sqrt{2}$ | $\frac{5}{2}$ | $\sqrt{4}$ |
| 4 | -2.3 | $-2\frac{1}{4}$ | $\frac{4}{2}$ | $-\frac{4}{2}$ | 2.09 |

Connections

42. **a.** Which of the triangles below are right triangles? Explain.

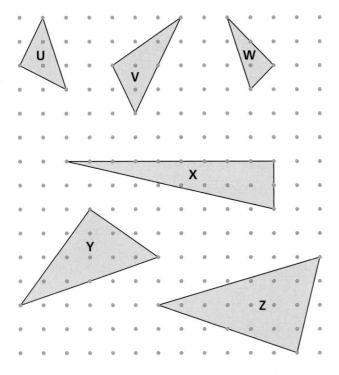

b. Find the area of each right triangle.

43. Refer to the squares you drew in Problem 2.1.

   a. Give the perimeter of each square to the nearest hundredth of a unit.

   b. What rule can you use to calculate the perimeter of a square if you know the length of a side?

44. On grid paper, draw coordinate axes like the ones below. Plot point P at $(1, -2)$.

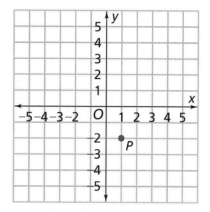

   a. Draw a square $PQRS$ with an area of 10 square units.

   b. Name a vertex of your square that is $\sqrt{10}$ units from point P.

   c. Give the coordinates of at least two other points that are $\sqrt{10}$ units from point P.

P needs to be a vertex of the square.

45. In Problem 2.3, you drew segments of length 1 unit, $\sqrt{2}$ units, 4 units, and so on. On a copy of the number line below, locate and label each length you drew. On the number line, $\sqrt{1}$ and $\sqrt{2}$ have been marked as examples.

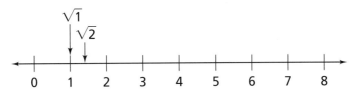

46. In Problem 2.1, it was easier to find the "upright" squares. Two of these squares are represented on the coordinate grid.

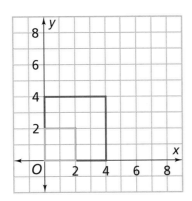

a. Are these squares similar? Explain.

b. How are the coordinates of the corresponding vertices related?

c. How are the areas of the squares related?

d. Copy the drawing. Add two more "upright" squares with a vertex at (0, 0). How are the coordinates of the vertices of these new squares related to the 2 × 2 square? How are their areas related?

Extensions

47. On dot paper, draw a non-rectangular parallelogram with an area of 6 square units.

48. On dot paper, draw a triangle with an area of 5 square units.

49. Dalida claims that $\sqrt{8} + \sqrt{8}$ is equal to $\sqrt{16}$ because 8 plus 8 is 16. Is she right? Explain.

50. The drawing shows three right triangles with a common side.

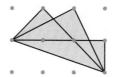

   a. Find the length of the common side.

   b. Do the three triangles have the same area? Explain.

We know that $\sqrt{5} \cdot \sqrt{5} = \sqrt{5 \cdot 5} = \sqrt{25} = 5$. Tell whether each product is a whole number. Explain.

51. $\sqrt{2} \cdot \sqrt{50}$

52. $\sqrt{4} \cdot \sqrt{16}$

53. $\sqrt{4} \cdot \sqrt{6}$

Mathematical Reflections 2

In this investigation, you explored squares and segments drawn on dot paper. You learned that the side length of a square is the positive square root of the square's area. You also discovered that, in many cases, a square root is not a whole number. These questions will help you summarize what you have learned.

Think about your answers to these questions. Discuss your ideas with other students and your teacher. Then write a summary of your findings in your notebook.

1. Describe how you would find the length of a line segment connecting two dots on dot paper. Be sure to consider horizontal, vertical, and tilted segments.

2. Explain what it means to find the square root of a number.

Investigation 3

The Pythagorean Theorem

Recall that a right triangle is a triangle with a right, or 90°, angle. The longest side of a right triangle is the side opposite the right angle. We call this side the **hypotenuse** of the triangle. The other two sides are called the **legs.** The right angle of a right triangle is often marked with a square.

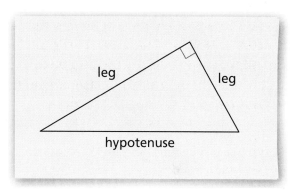

3.1 The Pythagorean Theorem

Each leg of the right triangle on the left below has a length of 1 unit. Suppose you draw squares on the hypotenuse and legs of the triangle, as shown on the right.

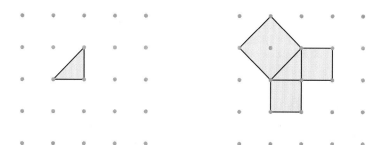

How are the areas of the three squares related?

In this problem, you will look for a relationship among the areas of squares drawn on the sides of right triangles.

A. Copy the table below. For each row of the table:

- Draw a right triangle with the given leg lengths on dot paper.

- Draw a square on each side of the triangle.

- Find the areas of the squares and record the results in the table.

Length of Leg 1 (units)	Length of Leg 2 (units)	Area of Square on Leg 1 (square units)	Area of Square on Leg 2 (square units)	Area of Square on Hypotenuse (square units)
1	1	1	1	2
1	2	▨	▨	▨
2	2	▨	▨	▨
1	3	▨	▨	▨
2	3	▨	▨	▨
3	3	▨	▨	▨
3	4	▨	▨	▨

B. Recall that a **conjecture** is your best guess about a mathematical relationship. It is usually a generalization about a pattern you think might be true, but that you do not yet know for sure is true.

For each triangle, look for a relationship among the areas of the three squares. Make a conjecture about the areas of squares drawn on the sides of any right triangle.

C. Draw a right triangle with side lengths that are different than those given in the table. Use your triangle to test your conjecture from Question B.

ACE Homework starts on page 38.

active math
online

For: Interactive Pythagoras
Visit: PHSchool.com
Web Code: apd-2300

The pattern you discovered in Problem 3.1 is a famous theorem named after the Greek mathematician Pythagoras. A *theorem* is a general mathematical statement that has been proven true. The Pythagorean Theorem is one of the most famous theorems in mathematics.

Over 300 different proofs have been given for the Pythagorean Theorem. One of these proofs is based on the geometric argument you will explore in this problem.

Did You Know?

Pythagoras lived in the sixth century B.C. He had a devoted group of followers known as the Pythagoreans.

The Pythagoreans were a powerful group. Their power and influence became so strong that some people feared they threatened the local political structure, and they were forced to disband. However, many Pythagoreans continued to meet in secret and to teach Pythagoras's ideas.

I had help!

PYTHAGORAS

Because they held Pythagoras in such high regard, the Pythagoreans gave him credit for all of their discoveries. Much of what we now attribute to Pythagoras, including the Pythagorean Theorem, may actually be the work of one or several of his followers.

Go Online
PHSchool.com
For: Information about Pythagoras
Web Code: ape-9031

Use the puzzles your teacher gives you.

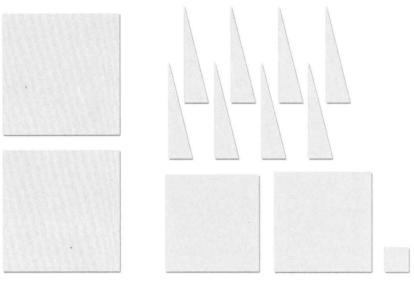

Puzzle frames   Puzzle pieces

A. Study a triangle piece and the three square pieces. How do the side lengths of the squares compare to the side lengths of the triangle?

B. 1. Arrange the 11 puzzle pieces to fit exactly into the two puzzle frames. Use four triangles in each frame.

2. What conclusion can you draw about the relationship among the areas of the three squares?

3. What does the conclusion you reached in part (2) mean in terms of the side lengths of the triangles?

4. Compare your results with those of another group. Did that group come to the same conclusion your group did? Is this conclusion true for all right triangles? Explain.

C. Suppose a right triangle has legs of length 3 centimeters and 5 centimeters.

1. Use your conclusion from Question B to find the area of a square drawn on the hypotenuse of the triangle.

2. What is the length of the hypotenuse?

D. In this Problem and Problem 3.1, you explored the Pythagorean Theorem, a relationship among the side lengths of a right triangle. State this theorem as a rule for any right triangle with leg lengths *a* and *b* and hypotenuse length *c*.

ACE **Homework starts on page 38.**

3.3 Finding Distances

In Investigation 2, you found the lengths of tilted segments by drawing squares and finding their areas. You can also find these lengths using the Pythagorean Theorem.

Problem 3.3 Finding Distances

In Questions A–D, refer to the grid below.

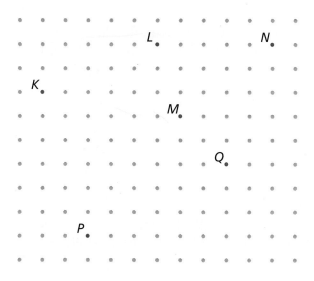

A. 1. Copy the points above onto dot paper. Draw a right triangle with segment *KL* as its hypotenuse.

2. Find the lengths of the legs of the triangle.

3. Use the Pythagorean Theorem to find the length of segment *KL*.

B. Find the distance between points *M* and *N* by connecting them with a segment and using the method in Question A.

C. Find the distance between points *P* and *Q*.

D. Find two points that are $\sqrt{13}$ units apart. Label the points *X* and *Y*. Explain how you know the distance between the points is $\sqrt{13}$ units.

ACE **Homework starts on page 38.**

You will now explore these questions about the Pythagorean Theorem:

- Is any triangle whose side lengths a, b, and c, satisfy the relationship $a^2 + b^2 = c^2$ a right triangle?

- Suppose the side lengths of a triangle do *not* satisfy the relationship $a^2 + b^2 = c^2$. Does this mean the triangle is *not* a right triangle?

Getting Ready for Problem 3.4

In ancient Egypt, the Nile River overflowed every year, flooding the surrounding lands and destroying property boundaries. As a result, the Egyptians had to remeasure their land every year.

Because many plots of land were rectangular, the Egyptians needed a reliable way to mark right angles. They devised a clever method involving a rope with equally spaced knots that formed 12 equal intervals.

To understand the Egyptians' method, mark off 12 segments of the same length on a piece of rope or string. Tape the ends of the string together to form a closed loop. Form a right triangle with side lengths that are whole numbers of segments.

- What are the side lengths of the right triangle you formed?
- Do the side lengths satisfy the relationship $a^2 + b^2 = c^2$?
- How do you think the Egyptians used the knotted rope?

Lengths That Form a Right Triangle

A. Copy the table below. Each row gives three side lengths. Use string, straws, or polystrips to build a triangle with the given side lengths. Then, complete the second and third columns of the table.

Side Lengths (units)	Do the side lengths satisfy $a^2 + b^2 = c^2$?	Is the triangle a right triangle?
3, 4, 5		
5, 12, 13		
5, 6, 10		
6, 8, 10		
4, 4, 4		
1, 2, 2		

B. 1. Make a conjecture about triangles whose side lengths satisfy the relationship $a^2 + b^2 = c^2$.

2. Make a conjecture about triangles whose side lengths do not satisfy the relationship $a^2 + b^2 = c^2$.

3. Check your conjecture with two other triangles. Explain why your conjecture will always be true.

C. Determine whether the triangle with the given side lengths is a right triangle.

1. 12 units, 16 units, 20 units

2. 8 units, 15 units, 17 units

3. 12 units, 9 units, 16 units

D. Which of these triangles are right triangles? Explain.

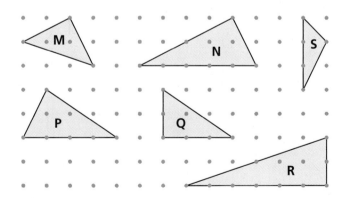

ACE Homework starts on page 38.

Applications

1. A right triangle has legs of length 5 inches and 12 inches.

   a. Find the area of a square drawn on the hypotenuse of the triangle.

   b. What is the length of the hypotenuse?

2. Use the Pythagorean Theorem to find the length of the hypotenuse of this triangle.

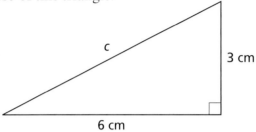

Homework
Help **●**nline
PHSchool.com
For: Help with Exercise 2
Web Code: ape-2302

3. On dot paper, find two points that are $\sqrt{17}$ units apart. Label the points W and X. Explain how you know the distance between the points is $\sqrt{17}$ units.

4. On dot paper, find two points that are $\sqrt{20}$ units apart. Label the points Y and Z. Explain how you know the distance between the points is $\sqrt{20}$ units.

Find the missing length(s).

5.

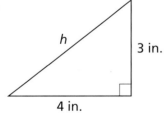

6.

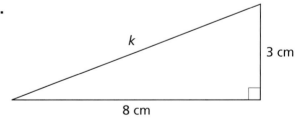

7.

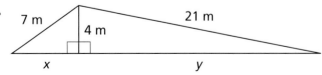

For Exercises 8–11, use the map of Euclid. Find the flying distance in blocks between the two landmarks without using a ruler. Explain.

8. greenhouse and stadium

9. police station and art museum

10. greenhouse and hospital

11. City Hall and gas station

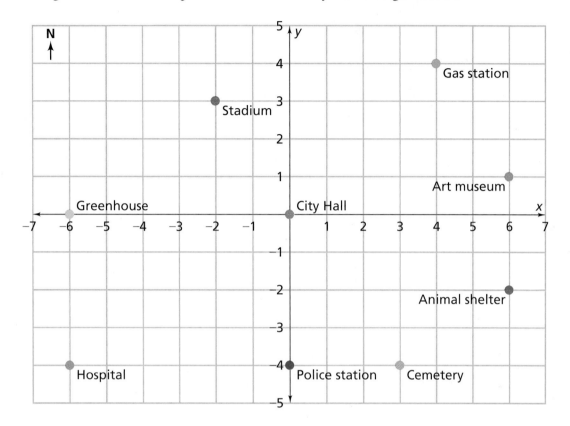

12. **Multiple Choice** Refer to the map above. Which landmarks are $\sqrt{40}$ blocks apart?

A. greenhouse and stadium

B. City Hall and art museum

C. hospital and art museum

D. animal shelter and police station

13. The diagram at the right shows a right triangle with a square on each side.

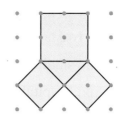

 a. Find the areas of the three squares.

 b. Use the areas from part (a) to show that this triangle satisfies the Pythagorean Theorem.

14. Show that this triangle satisfies the Pythagorean Theorem.

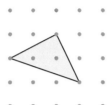

15. Multiple Choice Choose the set of side lengths that could make a right triangle.

 F. 10 cm, 24 cm, 26 cm   **G.** 4 cm, 6 cm, 10 cm

 H. 5 cm, 10 cm, $\sqrt{50}$ cm   **J.** 8 cm, 9 cm, 15 cm

Tell whether the triangle with the given side lengths is a right triangle.

16. 10 cm, 10 cm, $\sqrt{200}$ cm   **17.** 9 in., 16 in., 25 in.

Go Online
PHSchool.com

For: Multiple-Choice Skills Practice
Web Code: apa-2354

Connections

18. The prism at the right has a base that is a right triangle.

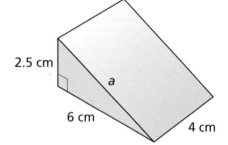

 a. What is the length of a?

 b. Do you need to know the length of a to find the volume of the prism? Do you need to know it to find the surface area? Explain.

 c. What is the volume?

 d. What is the surface area?

 e. Sketch a net for the prism.

For Exercises 19–22, refer to the figures below.

Cylinder

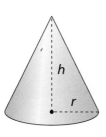
Cone

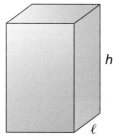
Prism

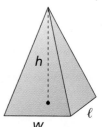
Pyramid

19. Multiple Choice Which expression represents the volume of the cylinder?

A. $2\pi r^2 + 2\pi rh$ **B.** $\pi r^2 h$ **C.** $\frac{1}{3}\pi r^2 h$ **D.** $\frac{1}{2}\pi r^2 h$

20. Multiple Choice Which expression represents the volume of the cone?

F. $2\pi r^2 + 2\pi rh$ **G.** $\pi r^2 h$ **H.** $\frac{1}{3}\pi r^2 h$ **J.** $\frac{1}{2}\pi r^2 h$

21. Multiple Choice Which expression represents the volume of the prism?

A. $2(\ell w + \ell h + wh)$ **B.** ℓwh

C. $\frac{1}{3}\ell wh$ **D.** $\frac{1}{2}\ell wh$

22. Multiple Choice Which expression represents the volume of the pyramid?

F. $2(\ell w + \ell h + wh)$ **G.** ℓwh

H. $\frac{1}{3}\ell wh$ **J.** $\frac{1}{2}\ell wh$

23. In the city of Euclid, Hilary's house is located at $(5, -3)$, and Jamilla's house is located at $(2, -4)$.

     a. Without plotting points, find the shortest driving distance in blocks between the two houses.

     b. What is the exact flying distance between the two houses?

24. Which labeled point is the same distance from point A as point B is from point A? Explain.

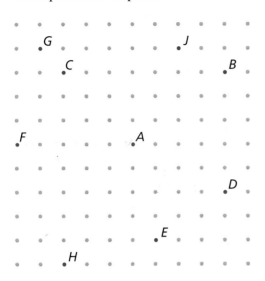

25. In the drawing at right, the cone and the cylinder have the same height and radius. Suppose the radius r of the cone is 2 units and the slant height d is $\sqrt{29}$ units.

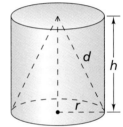

   a. What is the height of the cone?

   b. What is the volume of the cone?

26. In the drawing below, the pyramid and the cube have the same height and base.

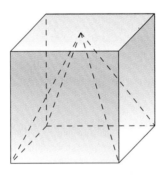

   a. Suppose the edge length of the cube is 6 units. What is the volume of the pyramid?

   b. Suppose the edge length of the cube is x units. What is the volume of the pyramid?

Extensions

27. Any tilted segment that connects two dots on dot paper can be the hypotenuse of a right triangle. You can use this idea to draw segments of a given length. The key is finding two square numbers with a sum equal to the square of the length you want to draw.

For example, suppose you want to draw a segment with length $\sqrt{5}$ units. You can draw a right triangle in which the sum of the areas of the squares on the legs is 5. The area of the square on the hypotenuse will be 5 square units, so the length of the hypotenuse will be $\sqrt{5}$ units. Because 1 and 4 are square numbers, and $1 + 4 = 5$, you can draw a right triangle with legs of lengths 1 and 2.

a. To use this method, it helps to be familiar with sums of square numbers. Copy and complete the addition table to show the sums of pairs of square numbers.

+	1	4	9	16	25	36	49	64
1	2	5						
4	5							
9								
16								
25								
36								
49								
64								

For parts (b)–(d) find two square numbers with the given sum.

   b. 10   **c.** 25   -   **d.** 89

For parts (e)–(h), draw tilted segments with the given lengths on dot paper. Use the addition table to help you. Explain your work.

   e. $\sqrt{26}$ units   **f.** 10 units

   g. $\sqrt{10}$ units   **h.** $\sqrt{50}$ units

For Exercises 28–33, tell whether it is possible to draw a segment of the given length by connecting dots on dot paper. Explain.

28. $\sqrt{2}$ units   **29.** $\sqrt{3}$ units   **30.** $\sqrt{4}$ units

31. $\sqrt{5}$ units   **32.** $\sqrt{6}$ units   **33.** $\sqrt{7}$ units

34. Ryan looks at the diagram below. He says, "If the center of this circle is at the origin, then I can figure out the radius."

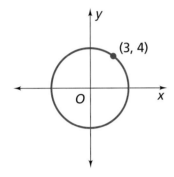

   a. Explain how Ryan can find the radius.

   b. What is the radius?

35. Use the graph to answer parts (a)–(c).

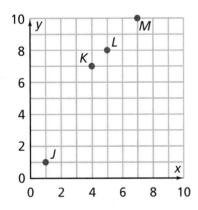

   a. Find the coordinates of *J* and *K*.

   b. Use the coordinates to find the distance from *J* to *K*. Explain your method.

   c. Use your method from part (b) to find the distance from *L* to *M*.

Mathematical Reflections 3

In this investigation, you worked with a very important mathematical relationship called the Pythagorean Theorem. These questions will help you summarize what you have learned.

Think about your answers to these questions. Discuss your ideas with other students and your teacher. Then write a summary of your findings in your notebook.

1. Suppose you are given the lengths of two sides of a right triangle. Describe how you can find the length of the third side.

2. Suppose two points on a grid are not on the same horizontal or vertical line. Describe how you can use the Pythagorean Theorem to find the distance between the points without measuring.

3. How can you determine whether a triangle is a right triangle if you know only the lengths of its sides?

Using the Pythagorean Theorem

In Investigation 3, you studied the Pythagorean Theorem, which states:

> The area of the square on the hypotenuse of a right triangle is equal to the sum of the areas of the squares on the legs.

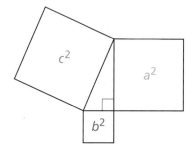

$$a^2 + b^2 = c^2$$

In this investigation, you will explore some interesting applications of the Pythagorean Theorem.

4.1 Analyzing The Wheel of Theodorus

The diagram on the next page is named for its creator, Theodorus of Cyrene (sy ree nee), a former Greek colony. Theodorus was a Pythagorean.

The Wheel of Theodorus begins with a triangle with legs 1 unit long and winds around counterclockwise. Each triangle is drawn using the hypotenuse of the previous triangle as one leg and a segment of length 1 unit as the other leg. To make the Wheel of Theodorus, you need only know how to draw right angles and segments 1 unit long.

Wheel of Theodorus

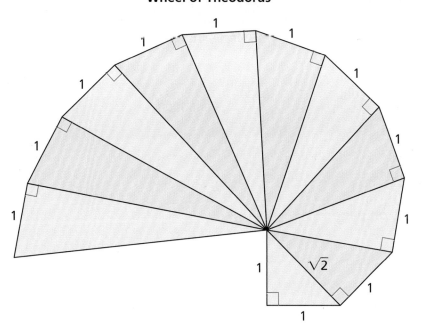

Problem 4.1 Analyzing the Wheel of Theodorus

A. Use the Pythagorean Theorem to find the length of each hypotenuse in the Wheel of Theodorus. On a copy of the wheel, label each hypotenuse with its length. Use the $\sqrt{\ }$ symbol to express lengths that are not whole numbers.

B. Use a cut-out copy of the ruler below to measure each hypotenuse on the wheel. Label the place on the ruler that represents the length of each hypotenuse. For example, the first hypotenuse length would be marked like this:

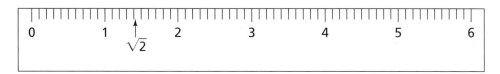

C. For each hypotenuse length that is not a whole number:

1. Give the two consecutive whole numbers the length is between. For example, $\sqrt{2}$ is between 1 and 2.

2. Use your ruler to find two decimal numbers (to the tenths place) the length is between. For example $\sqrt{2}$ is between 1.4 and 1.5.

3. Use your calculator to estimate the value of each length and compare the result to the approximations you found in part (2).

D. Odakota uses his calculator to find $\sqrt{3}$. He gets 1.732050808. Geeta says this must be wrong because when she multiplies 1.732050808 by 1.732050808, she gets 3.000000001. Why do these students disagree?

 Homework starts on page 53.

Did You Know?

Some decimals, such as 0.5 and 0.3125, *terminate.* They have a limited number of digits. Other decimals, such as 0.3333 . . . and 0.181818 . . . , have a repeating pattern of digits that never ends.

Terminating or repeating decimals are called **rational numbers** because they can be expressed as *ratios* of integers.

$$0.5 = \frac{1}{2} \qquad 0.3125 = \frac{5}{16} \qquad 0.3333 \ldots = \frac{1}{3} \qquad 0.181818 \ldots = \frac{2}{11}.$$

Some decimals neither terminate nor repeat. The decimal representation of the number π starts with the digits 3.14159265 . . . and goes forever without any repeating sequence of digits. Numbers with non-terminating and non-repeating decimal representations are called **irrational numbers.** They cannot be expressed as ratios of integers.

The number $\sqrt{2}$ is an irrational number. You had trouble finding an exact terminating or repeating decimal representation for $\sqrt{2}$ because such a representation does not exist. Other irrational numbers are $\sqrt{3}$, $\sqrt{5}$, and $\sqrt{11}$. In fact, $\sqrt{n}$ is an irrational number for any value of n that is not a square number.

The set of irrational and rational numbers is called the set of **real numbers.** An amazing fact about irrational numbers is that there is an infinite number of them between any two fractions!

4.2 Stopping Sneaky Sally

You can use the Pythagorean Theorem to solve problems in which you need to find the length of a side of a right triangle.

Problem 4.2 Finding Unknown Side Lengths

Horace Hanson is the catcher for the Humboldt Bees baseball team. Sneaky Sally Smith, the star of the Canfield Cats, is on first base. Sally is known for stealing bases, so Horace is keeping an eye on her.

The pitcher throws a fastball, and the batter swings and misses. Horace catches the pitch and, out of the corner of his eye, he sees Sally take off for second base.

Use the diagram to answer Questions A and B.

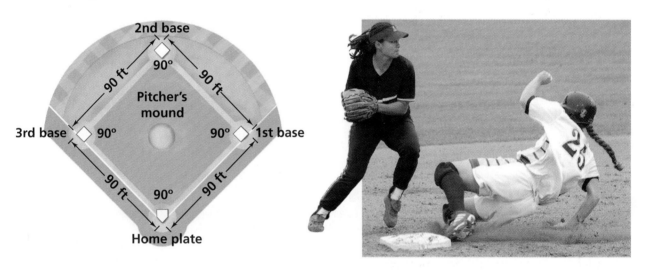

A. How far must Horace throw the baseball to get Sally out at second base? Explain.

B. The shortstop is standing on the baseline, halfway between second base and third base. How far is the shortstop from Horace?

C. The pitcher's mound is 60 feet 6 inches from home plate. Use this information and your answer to Question A to find the distance from the pitcher's mound to each base.

ACE Homework starts on page 53.

Although most people consider baseball an American invention, a similar game, called *rounders*, was played in England as early as the 1600s. Like baseball, rounders involved hitting a ball and running around bases. However, in rounders, the fielders actually threw the ball at the base runners. If a ball hit a runner while he was off base, he was out.

Alexander Cartwright was a founding member of the Knickerbockers Base Ball Club of New York City, baseball's first organized club. Cartwright played a key role in writing the first set of formal rules for baseball in 1845.

According to Cartwright's rules, a batter was out if a fielder caught the ball either on the fly or on the first bounce. Today, balls caught on the first bounce are not outs. Cartwright's rules also stated that the first team to have 21 runs at the end of an inning was the winner. Today, the team with the highest score after nine innings wins the game.

Go Online
PHSchool.com
For: Information about Alexander Cartwright
Web Code: ape-9031

4.3 Analyzing Triangles

All equilateral triangles have reflection symmetries. This property and the Pythagorean Theorem can be used to investigate some interesting properties of other equilateral triangles.

Getting Ready for Problem 4.3

Triangle ABC is an equilateral triangle.

- What is true about the angle measures in an equilateral triangle?
- What is true about the side lengths of an equilateral triangle?

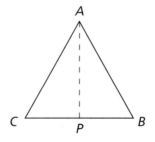

Line *AP* is a reflection line for triangle *ABC*.

- What can you say about the measures of the following angles? Explain.

    Angle *CAP*   Angle *BAP*

    Angle *CPA*   Angle *BPA*

- What can you say about line segments *CP* and *PB*? Explain.

- What can you say about triangles *ACP* and *ABP*?

Problem (4.3) Analyzing Triangles

A. Copy triangle *ABC* on the facing page. If the lengths of the sides of this equilateral triangle are 4 units, label the following measures:

1. angle *CAP*   **2.** angle *BAP*

3. angle *CPA*   **4.** angle *BPA*

5. length of *CP*   **6.** length of *PB*

7. length of *AP*

B. Suppose the lengths of the sides of *ABC* triangles are *s* units. Find the measures of the following:

1. angle *CAP*   **2.** angle *BAP*

3. angle *CPA*   **4.** angle *BPA*

5. length of *CP*   **6.** length of *PB*

7. length of *AP*

C. A right triangle with a 60° angle is called a 30-60-90 triangle. This 30-60-90 triangle has a hypotenuse of length 6 units.

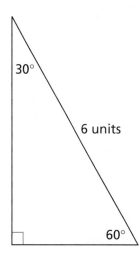

1. What are the lengths of the other two sides? Explain how you found your answers.

2. What relationships among the side lengths do you observe for this 30-60-90 triangle? Is this relationship true for all 30-60-90 triangles? Explain.

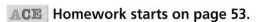

ACE Homework starts on page 53.

In this problem, you will apply many of the strategies you have developed in this unit, especially what you found in Problem 4.3.

Problem 4.4 Finding the Perimeter

Use the diagram for Questions A–C. Explain your work.

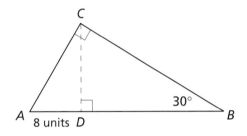

A. Find the perimeter of triangle ABC.

B. Find the area of triangle ABC.

C. Find the areas of triangle ACD and triangle BCD.

ACE Homework starts on page 53.

Did You Know?

In the movie *The Wizard of Oz,* the scarecrow celebrates his new brain by reciting the following:

"The sum of the square roots of any two sides of an isosceles triangle is equal to the square root of the remaining side."

Now you know what the scarecrow meant to say, even though his still imperfect brain got it wrong!

Applications

1. The hypotenuse of a right triangle is 15 centimeters long. One leg is 9 centimeters long. How long is the other leg?

2. The Wheel of Theodorus in Problem 4.1 includes only the first 11 triangles in the wheel. The wheel can go on forever.

   a. Find the side lengths of the next three triangles.

   b. Find the areas of the first five triangles in the wheel. Do you observe any pattern?

   c. Suppose you continue adding triangles to the wheel. Which triangle will have a hypotenuse of length 5 units?

In Exercises 3 and 4, find the missing length.

3.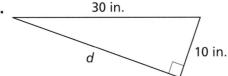

4.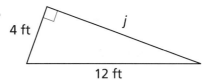

5. Moesha, a college student, needs to walk from her dorm room in Wilson Hall to her math class in Wells Hall. Normally, she walks 500 meters east and 600 meters north along the sidewalks, but today she is running late. She decides to take the shortcut through the Tundra.

   a. How many meters long is Moesha's shortcut?

   b. How much shorter is the shortcut than Moesha's usual route?

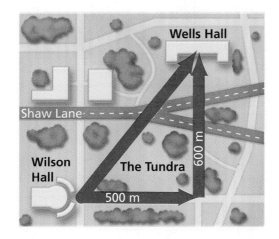

Investigation 4 Using the Pythagorean Theorem **53**

6. Square *ABCD* has sides of length 1 unit. The diagonal *BD* is a line of reflection.

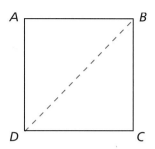

    a. How do the triangles *ABD* and *BDC* compare?

    b. Find the angle measures for one of the triangles. Explain how you found each measure.

    c. What is the length of the diagonal? Explain.

    d. Suppose square *ABCD* had sides of length 5 units instead of 1 unit. How would this change your answers to parts (b) and (c)?

7. A right triangle with a 45° angle is called a 45-45-90 triangle.

    a. Are all 45-45-90 triangles similar to each other? Explain.

    b. Suppose one leg of a 45-45-90 triangle is 5 units long. Find the perimeter of the triangle.

8. The diagram shows an amusement park ride in which tram cars glide along a cable. How long, to the nearest tenth of a meter, is the cable for the ride?

Not drawn to scale

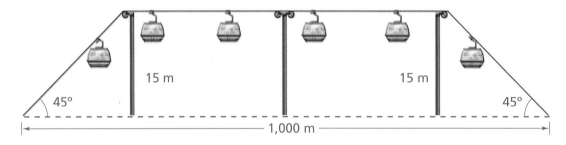

9. At Emmit's Evergreen Farm, the taller trees are braced by wires. A wire extends from 2 feet below the top of a tree to a stake in the ground. What is the tallest tree that can be braced with a 25-foot wire staked 15 feet from the base of the tree?

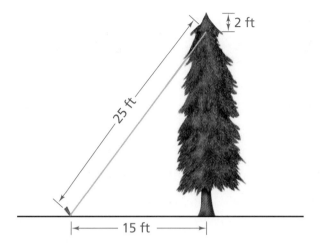

10. As part of his math assignment, Denzel has to estimate the height of a tower. He decides to use what he knows about 30-60-90 triangles.

Denzel makes the measurements shown below. About how tall is the tower? Explain.

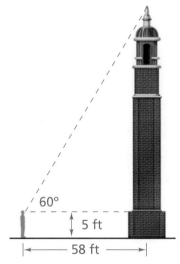

Not drawn to scale

11. a. Name all the 30-60-90 triangles in the figure below. Are all of these triangles similar to each other? Explain.

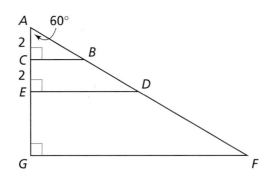

b. Find the ratio of the length of segment *BA* to the length of segment *AC*. What can you say about the corresponding ratio in the other 30-60-90 triangles?

c. Find the ratio of the length of segment *BC* to the length of segment *AC*. What can you say about the corresponding ratios in the other 30-60-90 triangles?

d. Find the ratio of the length of segment *BC* to the length of segment *AB*. What can you say about the corresponding ratios in the other 30-60-90 triangles?

e. Suppose the shortest side of a 30-60-90 triangle is 12 units long. Find the lengths of its other sides.

12. Find the perimeter of triangle *KLM*.

Homework
Help ⬤nline
PHSchool.com
For: Help with Exercise 12
Web Code: ape-2412

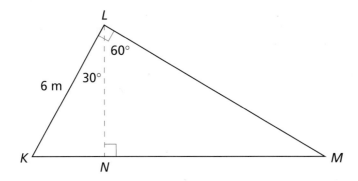

Connections

Go Online
PHSchool.com

For: Multiple-Choice Skills Practice
Web Code: apa-2454

Estimate the square root to one decimal place *without* using the $\sqrt{}$ key on your calculator. Then, tell whether the number is rational or irrational.

13. $\sqrt{121}$ **14.** $\sqrt{0.49}$ **15.** $\sqrt{15}$ **16.** $\sqrt{1{,}000}$

Two cars leave the city of Walleroo at noon. One car travels north and the other travels east. Use this information for Exercises 17 and 18.

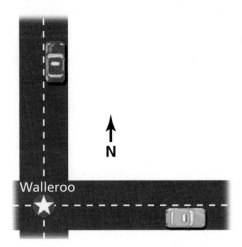

17. Suppose the northbound car is traveling at 60 miles per hour and the eastbound car is traveling at 50 miles per hour. Make a table that shows the distance each car has traveled and the distance between the two cars after 1 hour, 2 hours, 3 hours, and so on. Describe how the distances are changing.

18. Suppose the northbound car is traveling at 40 miles per hour. After 2 hours, the cars are 100 miles apart. How fast is the other car going? Explain.

Write each fraction as a decimal and tell whether the decimal is terminating or repeating. If the decimal is repeating, tell which digits repeat.

19. $\frac{2}{5}$ **20.** $\frac{3}{8}$ **21.** $\frac{5}{6}$ **22.** $\frac{35}{10}$ **23.** $\frac{8}{99}$

Tell whether a triangle with the given side lengths is a right triangle. Explain how you know.

24. 5 cm, 7 cm, $\sqrt{74}$ cm   **25.** $\sqrt{2}$ ft, $\sqrt{7}$ ft, 3 ft

26. The figure at the right is a net for a pyramid.

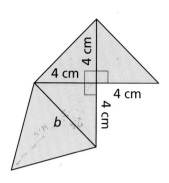

    a. What is the length of side b?

    b. Sketch the pyramid.

    c. What is the surface area of the pyramid?

27. Multiple Choice Which set of irrational numbers is in order from least to greatest?

    A. $\sqrt{2}, \sqrt{5}, \sqrt{11}, \pi$ **B.** $\sqrt{2}, \sqrt{5}, \pi, \sqrt{11}$

    C. $\sqrt{2}, \pi, \sqrt{5}, \sqrt{11}$ **D.** $\pi, \sqrt{2}, \sqrt{5}, \sqrt{11}$

28. In Problem 4.3, you found the side lengths of the triangle on the left.

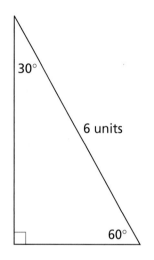

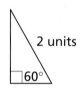

    a. Explain how you know the triangle on the right is similar to the triangle on the left.

    b. Use the side lengths of the larger triangle to find the side lengths of the smaller triangle. Explain.

    c. How are the areas of the triangles related?

Find a fraction equivalent to the terminating decimal.

29. 0.35 **30.** 2.1456 **31.** 89.050

For Exercises 32–34, tell whether the statement is *true* or *false*.

32. $0.06 = \sqrt{0.36}$ **33.** $1.1 = \sqrt{1.21}$ **34.** $20 = \sqrt{40}$

35. In Problem 4.4, you worked with this triangle.

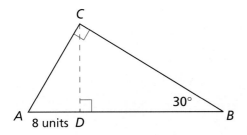

a. Find the perimeter of triangle *ACD*.

b. How is the perimeter of triangle *ACD* related to the perimeter of triangle *ABC*?

c. How is the area of triangle *ACD* related to the area of triangle *ABC*?

Find the two consecutive whole numbers the square root is between. Explain.

36. $\sqrt{39}$

37. $\sqrt{600}$

Extensions

38. a. Copy the table at the right. Write each fraction as a decimal.

b. Describe a pattern you see in your table.

c. Use the pattern to write decimal representations for $\frac{9}{9}$, $\frac{10}{9}$, and $\frac{15}{9}$. Use your calculator to check your answers.

d. Find fractions equivalent to $1.\overline{2}$ and $2.\overline{7}$, where the bar means the number under the bar repeats forever. (**Hint:** $1.\overline{2}$ can be written as $1 + 0.22222...$ The bar on the 2 means the 2 repeats forever.)

Fraction	Decimal
$\frac{1}{9}$	
$\frac{2}{9}$	
$\frac{3}{9}$	
$\frac{4}{9}$	
$\frac{5}{9}$	
$\frac{6}{9}$	
$\frac{7}{9}$	
$\frac{8}{9}$	

39. Explore decimal representations of fractions with a denominator of 99. Look at fractions less than one, $\frac{1}{99}, \frac{2}{99}, \frac{3}{99}$, and so on. What patterns do you see?

40. Explore decimal representations of fractions with a denominator of 999. Look at fractions less than one, $\frac{1}{999}, \frac{2}{999}, \frac{3}{999}$, and so on. What patterns do you see?

Use the patterns you discovered in Exercises 38–40 to find a fraction or mixed number equivalent to each decimal.

41. 0.3333 . . .   **42.** 0.050505 . . .   **43.** 0.454545 . . .

44. 0.045045 . . .   **45.** 10.121212 . . .   **46.** 3.9999 . . .

For Exercises 47 and 48, find the length of the diagonal *d*.

47.

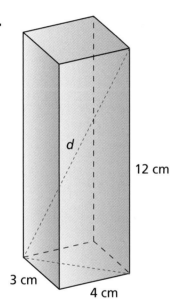

48.

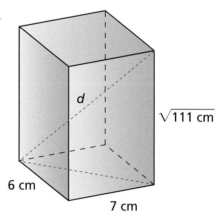

49. Segment *AB* below makes a 45° angle with the *x*-axis. The length of segment *AB* is 5 units.

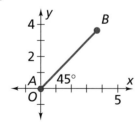

   a. Find the coordinates of point *B* to two decimal places.

   b. What is the slope of line *AB*?

In Exercises 50–52, you will look for relationships among the areas of similar shapes other than squares drawn on the sides of a right triangle.

50. Half-circles have been drawn on the sides of this right triangle.

    a. Find the area of each half-circle.

    b. How are the areas of the half-circles related?

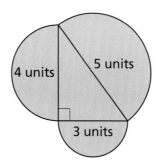

51. Equilateral triangles have been drawn on the sides of this right triangle.

    a. Find the area of each equilateral triangle.

    b. How are the areas of the equilateral triangles related?

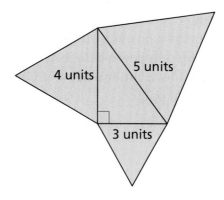

52. Regular hexagons have been drawn on the sides of this right triangle.

    a. Find the area of each hexagon.

    b. How are the areas of the hexagons related?

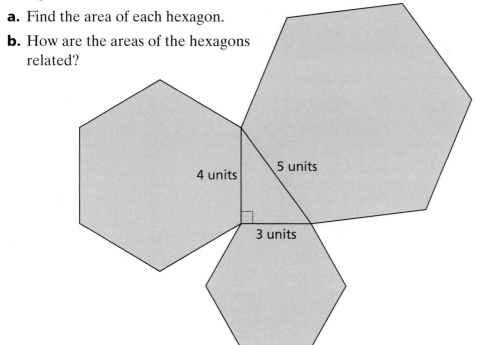

53. Find an irrational number between 6.23 and 6.35.

54. You can use algebra to help you write a repeating decimal as a fraction. For example, suppose you want to write 0.12121212 . . . as a fraction.

Let $x = 0.12121212 \ldots$.

$100x = 12.12121212 \ldots$ Multiply both sides by 100.

$- x = 0.12121212 \ldots$ Subtract the first equation from the second.

$\overline{99x = 12}$

Divide both sides of the resulting equation, $99x = 12$, by 99 to get $x = \frac{12}{99}$. So, $0.12121212 \ldots = \frac{12}{99}$.

The key to this method is to multiply each side of the original equation by a power of 10 (such, as 10, 100, or 1,000) that shifts one group of repeating digits to the left of the decimal point. In the example above, multiplying by 100 shifted one "12" to the left of the decimal point.

Use the method described above to write each decimal as a fraction.

a. $0.\,15151515 \ldots$ **b.** $0.\,7777 \ldots$ **c.** $0.123123123123 \ldots$

55. When building a barn, a farmer must make sure the sides are perpendicular to the ground.

a. One method for checking whether a wall is perpendicular to the ground involves using a 10-foot pole. The farmer makes a mark exactly 6 feet high on the wall. She then places one end of the pole on the mark and the other end on the ground.

How far from the base of the wall will the pole touch the ground if the wall is perpendicular to the ground? Explain.

b. You may have heard the saying, "I wouldn't touch that with a 10-foot pole!" What would this saying mean to a farmer who had just built a barn?

c. Suppose a farmer uses a 15-foot pole and makes a mark 12 feet high on the wall. How far from the base of the wall will the pole touch the ground if the wall is perpendicular to the ground?

d. Name another pole length a farmer could use. For this length how high should the mark on the wall be? How far from the base of the wall will the pole touch the ground?

56. Find the perimeter of triangle *ABC*.

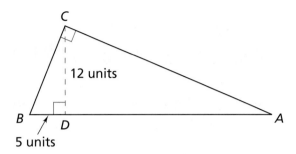

57. Below is the net for a square pyramid and a sketch of the pyramid.

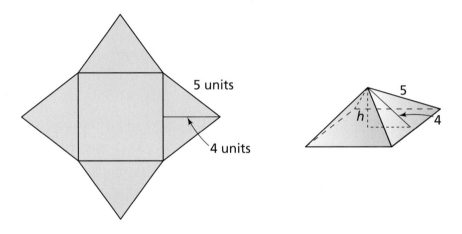

a. What is the area of the base of the pyramid?

b. What is the surface area of the pyramid?

c. What is the height of the pyramid?

d. What is the volume of the pyramid?

58. The managers of Izzie's Ice Cream Shop are trying to decide on the best size for their cones.

a. Izzie thinks the cone should have a diameter of 4.5 inches and a height of 6 inches. What is the volume of the cone Izzie suggests?

b. Izzie's sister Becky thinks the cone should have a height of 6 inches and a slant height of 7 inches. (The slant height is labeled *s* in the diagram at the right.) What is the volume of the cone Becky suggests?

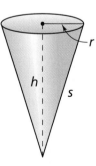

Mathematical Reflections 4

In this investigation, you applied the ideas from the first three investigations. The following questions will help you summarize what you have learned.

Think about your answers to these questions. Discuss your ideas with other students and your teacher. Then write a summary of your findings in your notebook.

1. In what ways is the Pythagorean Theorem useful? Give at least two examples.

2. Describe the special properties of a 30-60-90 triangle.

Looking Back and Looking Ahead

While working on problems in this unit, you extended your skill in using a coordinate system to locate points and figures. Then, by studying patterns in the side lengths and areas of squares on dot grids, you learned the Pythagorean Theorem. You used this property of right triangles to solve a variety of practical problems, some of which involved irrational numbers.

Go Online
PHSchool.com
For: Vocabulary Review Puzzle
Web Code: apj-2051

Use Your Understanding: The Pythagorean Theorem

Test your understanding of the Pythagorean Theorem and its relationship to area, lengths of line segments, and irrational numbers by solving the following problems.

1. The diagram shows a Chinese tangram puzzle on a 10-by-10 grid.

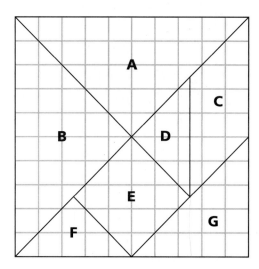

    a. What is the area of shape E?

    b. What is the length of each side of shape E?

    c. What are the lengths of the sides of triangle A?

    d. Name all the triangles that are similar to triangle A. In each case, give a scale factor for the similarity relationship.

2. A 60-foot piece of wire is strung between the top of a tower and the ground, making a 30-60-90 triangle.

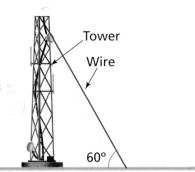

Tower

Wire

60°

    a. How far from the center of the base of the tower is the wire attached to the ground?

    b. How high is the tower?

Explain Your Reasoning

When you present work based on the Pythagorean relationship, you should be able to justify your calculations and conclusions.

    3. How can you find the side length of a square if you know its area?

    4. How can you find the length of a segment joining two points on a coordinate grid?

    5. The diagrams below show squares drawn on the sides of triangles.

Figure 1   **Figure 2**

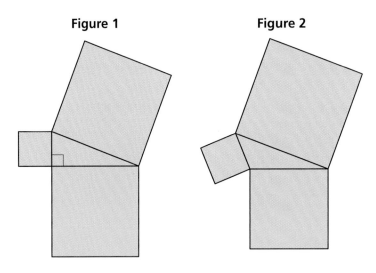

    a. In Figure 1, what is the relationship among the areas of the squares?

    b. Explain why the relationship you describe in part (a) is not true for Figure 2.

6. Explain with words and symbols how to use the Pythagorean Theorem to find the

   a. length of a diagonal of a square with side length s.

   b. length of a diagonal of a rectangle with side lengths s and t.

   c. length of the hypotenuse of a right triangle with legs of lengths s and t.

   d. height of an equilateral triangle with side length s.

   e. length of one leg of a triangle when the lengths of the hypotenuse and the other leg are h and t, respectively.

Look Ahead

You will use the properties of right triangles you discovered in this unit, including the Pythagorean Theorem, in many future *Connected Mathematics* units, and in the math, science, and technology courses you take in high school and college.

English/Spanish Glossary

C

conjecture A guess about a pattern or relationship based on observations.

conjetura Suposición acerca de un patron o relación, basada en observaciones.

H

hypotenuse The side of a right triangle that is opposite the right angle. The hypotenuse is the longest side of a right triangle. In the triangle below, the side labeled *c* is the hypotenuse.

hipotenusa El lado de un triángulo rectángulo que está opuesto al ángulo recto. La hipotenusa es el lado más largo de un triángulo rectángulo. En el triángulo de abajo, el lado rotulado *c* es la hipotenusa.

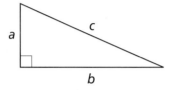

I

irrational number A number that cannot be written as a fraction with a numerator and a denominator that are integers. The decimal representation of an irrational number never ends and never shows a repeating pattern of a fixed number of digits. The numbers $\sqrt{2}$, $\sqrt{3}$, $\sqrt{5}$, and π are examples of irrational numbers.

número irracional Un número que no puede escribirse como una fracción con un numerador y un denominador que sean enteros. La representación decimal de un número irracional nunca termina y nunca muestra un patrón de dígitos que se repite. Los números $\sqrt{2}$, $\sqrt{3}$, $\sqrt{5}$, y π son ejemplos de números irracionales.

L

legs The sides of a right triangle that are adjacent to the right angle. In the triangle above, the sides labeled *a* and *b* are the legs.

catetos Los lados de un triángulo rectángulo que son adyacentes al ángulo recto. En el triángulo de arriba, los lados *a* y *b* son los catetos.

P

perpendicular Forming a right angle. For example, the sides of a right triangle that form the right angle are perpendicular.

perpendicular Que forma un ángulo recto. Por ejemplo, los lados de un triángulo rectángulo que forman el ángulo recto son perpendiculares.

Pythagorean Theorem A statement about the relationship among the lengths of the sides of a right triangle. The theorem states that if *a* and *b* are the lengths of the legs of a right triangle and *c* is the length of the hypotenuse, then $a^2 + b^2 = c^2$.

Teorema de Pitágoras Un enunciado acerca de la relación que existe entre las longitudes de los lados de un triángulo rectángulo. El teorema enuncia que si *a* y *b* son las longitudes de los catetos de un triángulo rectángulo y *c* es la longitud de la hipotenusa, entonces $a^2 + b^2 = c^2$.

rational number A number that can be written as a fraction with a numerator and a denominator that are integers. The decimal representation of a rational number either ends or repeats. Examples of rational numbers are $\frac{1}{2}$, $\frac{78}{91}$, 7, 0.2, and 0.191919. . . .

número racional Un número que puede escribirse como una fracción con un numerador y un denominador que son enteros. La representación decimal de un número racional termina o bien se repite. Ejemplos de números racionales son $\frac{1}{2}$, $\frac{78}{91}$, 7, 0.2 y 0.191919. . . .

real numbers The set of all rational numbers and all irrational numbers. The number line represents the set of real numbers.

números reales El conjunto de todos los números racionales y todos los números irracionales. La recta numérica representa el conjunto de los números reales.

repeating decimal A decimal with a pattern of a fixed number of digits that repeats forever, such as 0.3333333. . . and 0.73737373. . . . Repeating decimals are rational numbers.

decimal periódico Un decimal con un patrón de dígitos que se repite indefinidamente, como 0.3333333. . . y 0.73737373. . . . Los decimales que se repiten son números racionales.

square root If $A = s^2$, then s is the square root of A. For example, -3 and 3 are square roots of 9 because $3 \cdot 3 = 9$ and $-3 \cdot -3 = 9$. The $\sqrt{}$ symbol is used to denote the positive square root. So, we write $\sqrt{9} = 3$. The positive square root of a number is the side length of a square that has that number as its area. So, you can draw a segment of length $\sqrt{5}$ by drawing a square with an area of 5, and the side length of the square will be $\sqrt{5}$.

raíz cuadrada Si $A = s^2$, entonces s es la raíz cuadrada de A. Por ejemplo, -3 y 3 son raíces cuadradas de 9 porque $3 \cdot 3 = 9$ y $-3 \cdot -3 = 9$. El símbolo $\sqrt{}$ se usa para indicar la raíz cuadrada positiva. Por eso, escribimos $\sqrt{9} = 3$. La raíz cuadrada positiva de un número es la longitud del lado de un cuadrado que tiene dicho número como su área. Entonces, puedes dibujar un segmento de longitud $\sqrt{5}$ dibujando un cuadrado con un área de 5 y la longitud del lado del cuadrado será $\sqrt{5}$.

terminating decimal A decimal that ends, or terminates, such as 0.5 or 0.125. Terminating decimals are rational numbers.

decimal finito Un decimal que se acaba o termina, como 0.5 ó 0.125. Los decimales finitos son números racionales.

Academic Vocabulary

Academic vocabulary words are words that you see in textbooks and on tests. These are not math vocabulary terms, but knowing them will help you succeed in mathematics.

Las palabras de vocabulario académico son palabras que ves en los libros de texto y en las pruebas. Éstos no son términos de vocabulario de matemáticas, pero conocerlos te ayudará a tener éxito en matemáticas.

A

analyze To think about and understand facts and details about a given set of information. Analyzing can involve providing a written summary supported by factual information, a diagram, chart, table, or any combination of these.

related terms: explain, describe, justify

Sample: Analyze the squares. How is the side length related to the area?

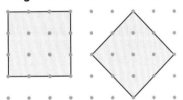

The first square has an area of 9 units^2 and a side length of 3 units. The side length is the square root of the area. The second square has an area of 4 full units^2 and 8 half-units^2 for a total of 8 units^2. The side length is the square root of the area or $\sqrt{8}$ units.

analizar Pensar acerca de y comprender hechos y detalles sobre un conjunto determinado de información. Analizar puede implicar proporcionar un resumen escrito apoyado por información real, un diagrama, una gráfica, una tabla o cualquier combinación de éstos.

términos relacionados: explicar, describir, justificar

Ejemplo: Analiza los cuadrados. ¿Cómo se relaciona la longitud del lado con el área?

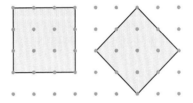

El primer cuadrado tiene un área de 9 unidades^2 y una longitud del lado de 3 unidades. La longitud del lado es la raíz cuadrada del área. El segundo cuadrado tiene un área de 4 unidades^2 completas y 8 unidades^2 medias que hacen un total de 8 unidades^2. La longitud del lado es la raíz cuadrada del área u $\sqrt{8}$ unidades.

E

estimate To find an approximate answer.
related terms: approximate, guess
Sample: Estimate $\sqrt{10}$.

I know that $\sqrt{9} = 3$ and $\sqrt{16} = 4$. Since $\sqrt{10}$ is much closer to $\sqrt{9}$ than it is to $\sqrt{16}$, my estimate will be closer to 3 than to 4. I estimate $\sqrt{10}$ as about 3.2.

estimar Hallar una respuesta aproximada.
términos relacionados: aproximar, conjeturar
Ejemplo: Estima $\sqrt{10}$.

Sé que $\sqrt{9} = 3$ y $\sqrt{16} = 4$. Puesto que $\sqrt{10}$ está mucho más cerca de $\sqrt{9}$ que de $\sqrt{16}$, mi estimación estaría más cercana a 3 que a 4. Estimo que $\sqrt{10}$ es aproximadamente de 3.2.

find To use the given information and any related facts, to determine or calculate a value. You may use mathematical algorithms, properties, formulas, or any combination of these, as well as other mathematical strategies, when finding a value.

related terms: calculate, discover, determine

Sample: Find the area of triangle *ABC*.

I can count the number of unit squares. △ABC has an area of 4.5 unit squares. I can also find the area by using the formula $A = \frac{1}{2}bh$, where the base and the height of the triangle are each 3 units in length.

$A = \frac{1}{2}(3)(3) = 4.5$ square units

hallar Usar la información dada y cualesquiera datos relacionados para determinar o calcular un valor. Puedes usar algoritmos matemáticos, propiedades, fórmulas o cualquier combinación de éstos, así como otras estrategias matemáticas, cuando hallas un valor.

términos relacionado: calcular, descubrir, determinar

Ejemplo: Halla el área del triángulo *ABC*.

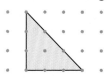

Puedo contar el número de unidades cuadradas. El △ABC tiene un área de 4.5 unidades cuadradas. Puedo hallar el área usando la fórmula $A = \frac{1}{2}ba$, donde la base y la altura del triángulo miden 3 unidades de longitud respectivamente.

$A = \frac{1}{2}(3)(3) = 4.5$ square units

observe To notice or to examine carefully one or more characteristics of a particular object.

related terms: notice, examine, note, see

Sample: What do you observe about the sum of the squares of the lengths of the legs of the right triangle in relationship to the length of the hypotenuse?

If I square the length of the hypotenuse, I get $5^2 = 25$. This is equal to the sum of the squares of the lengths of the legs of the triangle $3^2 + 4^2 = 9 + 16 = 25$.

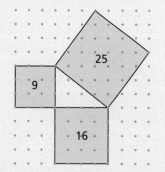

The area of the square built on the hypotenuse is equal to the sum of the areas of the squares built on the two legs of the right triangle.

observar Notar o examinar con cuidado una o más características de un objeto particular.

términos relacionados: k notar, examinar, señalar, ver

Ejemplo: ¿Qué observas sobre la suma de los cuadrados de las longitudes de los catetos del triángulo rectángulo con relación a la longitud de la hipotenusa?

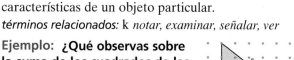

Si elevo al cuadrado la longitud de la hipotenusa, obtengo $5^2 = 25$. Esto es igual a la suma de los cuadrados de las longitudes de los catetos del triángulo $3^2 + 4^2 = 9 + 16 = 25$.

El área del cuadrado construido sobre la hipotenusa es igual a la suma de las áreas de los cuadrados construidos sobre los dos catetos del triángulo rectángulo.

Academic Vocabulary

Index

Index

Acknowledgments

Team Credits

The people who made up the **Connected Mathematics 2** team—representing editorial, editorial services, design services, and production services—are listed below. Bold type denotes core team members.

Leora Adler, Judith Buice, Kerry Cashman, Patrick Culleton, Sheila DeFazio, Katie Hallahan, Richard Heater, **Barbara Hollingdale, Jayne Holman,** Karen Holtzman, **Etta Jacobs,** Christine Lee, Carolyn Lock, Catherine Maglio, **Dotti Marshall,** Rich McMahon, Eve Melnechuk, Kristin Mingrone, Terri Mitchell, **Marsha Novak,** Irene Rubin, Donna Russo, Robin Samper, Siri Schwartzman, **Nancy Smith,** Emily Soltanoff, **Mark Tricca,** Paula Vergith, Roberta Warshaw, Helen Young

Additional Credits

Diana Bonfilio, Mairead Reddin, Michael Torocsik, nSight, Inc.

Technical Illustration

WestWords, Inc.

Cover Design

tom white.images

Photos

2, Erich Lessing/Art Resource, NY; **3,** Yellow Dog Productions/Getty Images, Inc.; **5,** Francis Miller/Time Life Pictures; **6,** Richard T Nowitz/Getty Images, Inc.; **15,** Comstock Images/Getty Images, Inc.; **20,** Richard Haynes; **27,** Richard Haynes; **28,** Catherine Ledner/Getty Images, Inc.; **33,** The Art Archive/Museo Capitolino Rome/Dagli Orti (A); **36,** Erich Lessing/Art Resource, NY; **41 both,** Richard Haynes; **44,** Richard Haynes; **46,** Patrick Ben Luke Syder/Lonely Planet Images; **49,** AP Photo/Jerry Laizure; **50,** Library of Congress, Prints and Photographs Division, LOT 13163-09, no. 1; **52,** Courtesy Everett Collection/ Everett Collection; **54,** Dennis MacDonald/Photo Edit

Data Sources

Did You Know quote on page 52 is an excerpt from *The Wizard of Oz* granted courtesy of Warner Bros. Entertainment Inc. All Rights Reserved. Copyright © 1939.

Note: Every effort has been made to locate the copyright owner of the material reprinted in this book. Omissions brought to our attention will be corrected in subsequent editions.